Real Dogs Don't Whisper

Life lessons from a larger than life dog - and his owner!

By

Kelly Preston

&

Mr. MaGoo

Dedication

Kelly's

I want to thank my family and friends that have inspired, supported, and motivated me to write this book. I also would like to give thanks to all the beautiful pets that I have (and had) and the priceless lessons they taught me; guiding me and encouraging me to grow.

God, thank-you for being in the center of my life, truly blessing me with a wonderful family, supporting friends; and, entrusting me with the lives of the pets that You have graced me with (both past and present).

Dad, I love you and thank you for believing in me.

Mr MaGoo's

Woof! Woof! I want to send a big thank-you to all the pet parents and rescue organizations; without you, pets like my siblings would not be given a second chance in life. Thank you for all the invaluable work you do; and dedication, love and patience you provide. *Woof! Woof!*

Preface

Two women walk into a bar.

1st Woman: I'm afraid I'm going to have to get rid of my dog.

2nd Woman: Why? I thought you loved that dog.

1st Woman: I do love him. The dog sings and dances and tells jokes. The problem is that the dog recently told me his life had been so good, he wants to write a book about it. Now I can't get the darned thing off my computer.

2nd Woman: Your dog knows how to use a computer?

That's my nine year old Lhasa Apso and co-writer, Mr. MaGoo (Handsome Goo). He tells that joke all the time. Such a handful and yet a fabulous little writer with a unique perspective on our uncommon family (though Mr. MaGoo and I most certainly don't always agree).

Then there's Betty Boop (BoopBoopDiBoop), my ten year old designer breed/mutt. Betty Boop came to me with severe neurological disorders. Her fate has been uncertain, at best. But she remains a living, breathing miracle in our lives today.

Next we have Buffy (Beautiful Buffy), my thirteen year old Cocker Spaniel. Buffy was rescued from an abusive home. Through patience and love, Buffy has become a more social and trusting pet. She is the eldest of the group, and in many ways, our canine matriarch.

And of course, there's Carla Mae (Cutie Cutie Carla Mae)—another nine year old Lhasa Apso. Sadly, Carla Mae's history is not a pretty picture either. However, the distance she has come is amazing.

With the help of Mr. MaGoo, I'd like to share with you one woman's journey raising and caring for four high-need dogs. It's been nothing less than a life-altering journey – a journey of self-discovery in the company of these wonderful, magical, frustrating, adorable, infuriating, always-loveable mates. My hope is that you will enjoy this sometimes funny, sometimes sad, sometimes outrageous tale as told by a human and her dog.

-Kelly Preston

Chapter One

The Legend Begins

It's a dog's life. What in the world does *that* mean? I'm a dog and even I don't know what it means.

Allow me to introduce myself: I am the alpha and omega of all dogs – in the cutest and sparkiest, most fun-loving package ever. Oh yeah. Watch me strut! Appreciate the butt. Too cute, right? *Woof!* They call me "Mr. MaGoo." Sometimes "Goo," "Good Boy," "Handsome Boy," and occasionally "Dammit Goo!"

The statement, "It's a dog's life," somehow seems to imply that all dogs are alike or share a common dog-life experience. No doubt the words of a human, as nothing could be further from the truth. What is "the truth?" you ask. Get comfortable kids. I will share with you my vast knowledge of The Truth. But buckle up. It's bound to be a bumpy ride.

The Truth: All dogs are not alike. Some of us are born to lead while others (like my sisters and the human who lives in my house) are born to follow. They are indeed quite fortunate to have such an irresistibly cute leader who is, quite simply (and humbly), the single best Alpha Dog of all time. I am protector and ruler of my home and my neighborhood.

ARRRF! ARF! ARF! That's right, Sparky, just keep on moving. Your yard is down a couple houses in case you've forgotten.

Did you guys see that? Freaking Sparky out lingering in *my* front yard. Every day I am fiercely defending my home and family, providing outstanding guidance and direction in an otherwise chaotic environment, patiently teaching those around me (though my patience is often tried by the hard-headed human with whom we reside) —while remaining endlessly entertaining and uplifting all the while. Not to mention, I'm writing this book for crying out loud. How many dogs do you know with literary brilliance and mad computer skills?

WOOF! WOOOF! Car alert! Everybody down! WOOF! That's it clown—keep it moving. WOOF!

"Clown" is dog-speak for people who leave a funny taste in our mouths. We have seen our share of clowns around here. I have seen the human bravely set boundaries and boldly hold her ground with them. She sometimes refers to them as "gentlemen." I think she uses that term way too loosely.

Impressively so, I am an amazing leader and like to run a tight ship, which isn't always easy as these are some seriously-slacking individuals around this place. I live with my three sisters: Buffy, Betty Boop, and Carla Mae, along with a human who provides us with necessary goods and services. I am, rather obviously, the plenipotentiary of the household. It's a necessity.

I like to have everyone up and moving by 5 a.m., but often I find it takes until as late as 5:30 to accomplish my goal. *WOOF! Up and at 'em! Rise and shine!! Let's go troops! WOOF! Time to get a move on!* "It's too *early*," the human frequently whines. "Don't be so *loud!*" Yeah, right. Too early. Um… I think I know what time it is, mmkay? It's time to get up! What am I supposed to do? Whisper? I don't think so. I'm a *real* dog, thank you very much.

Anyway, once I get Buffy, Carla Mae, and the human down the stairs (Betty Boop stays on the lower level —so no worries there), I give them a good thirty to forty-five minutes to get up to speed and have my breakfast prepared before I join them in the kitchen. This time also allows me the opportunity to relax and reflect on the awesomeness that is me.

Then it's breakfast and time to round up the troops for a walk. *Arf!* The human grabs leashes and I line up Buffy and Carla Mae. *Woof!* Betty Boop stays in the house due to the fact that she is linearly challenged and only walks in circles. I say make the circles bigger and you can see the world. The human thinks she knows better. But there is no sense spending all my time fighting the little battles. I have plenty of big battles to take care of. Besides, the human is really kind of cute and can be fun when she is able to maintain some sort of focus. Oh! And the doggy treats! WOOOOOF! Can't forget the doggy treats. She always has the best doggy treats. Gotta give credit where credit is due.

Did I mention I am entirely cute? One step out the front door and the paparazzi are everywhere – *cl-click, cl-click, cl-click, cl-click.* That's right. Watch me walk. "I'm… too sexy for my leash… too sexy for my leash…" *WOOF! Back it up, Sparky. This is my photo op.* Oh yeah… break it down… watch me wiggle. March it out.

WOOOOF! A nice, long stretch of grass! GRASS! I love to run in the grass! C'mon girls! Try to keep up. Frolicking around the neighborhood and visiting with my loyal subjects rocks. I try to give 'em a thrill when I can. I'm an entertaining and playful companion. At first glance you are bound to be dazzled by my strength, leadership, and undeniable cuteness. But what's awesome about me doesn't end there. I am a *constant* source of fun. I sometimes amaze myself by all the energy I still have after a grueling day of protecting and organizing, and creating order out of perfect madness. Yet I still can put the "fun" in Funyuns at the end of the day. The world *is* a better and safer place because of me.

To say that all dogs are even remotely equal is ridiculous and a mathematical impossibility. Oh sure, in a perfect world all dogs would be as cute and fearless as me. Sadly though, that is not the case and the weight and responsibility of my world rests with me. But I'm tough and I can handle it. I come from a long line of prized, fearless, and amazingly cute Lhasa Apsos. My family tree dates back to 800 B.C. in some place called Tibet. We are the proud dogs that guarded castles and protected monasteries. Palaces relied on our keen hearing and remarkable ability to take charge of the other (often bigger) dogs. Our barks are known for the fear they instill in both man and beast. Back in the day you couldn't *buy* one of us if you were the wealthiest person on earth. No amount of treasure or gold or precious gems was considered to be adequate in exchange for such a priceless animal. We could only be *given* as gifts. Interestingly enough – Lhasa Apsos, to this very day, are considered by the entire universe to be a gift of the grandest proportion. So don't let me hear you call us "yappy rat dogs." That's just rude and offensive, not to mention grossly inaccurate. Our barks are fierce and our size is deceptive. We are the most regal dogs known to man. A "yappy rat dog?" I am a *gift*, and because I am so strong and sturdy and well-bred, I'll probably live forever too. I am the natural choice to protect my home and all those who reside here.

I suppose now might be a good time to tell you a little about my sisters. Bow-wow, what a handful! The term "high maintenance" comes to mind. Thankfully, the house is napping and the human is not home to kick me off the computer. ARF! Talk about "bossy." More about the human later.

Buffy is a lovely thirteen-year-old Cocker Spaniel and truly the lady of the house. She's somewhat aloof with a sophisticated air about her, though sometimes her fear of men and "other dogs" is confusing. She is only four years older than I, yet acts like she is 150. I cannot pretend to understand why *any* dog would not want to play with me. I'm cute. I'm fun. I like to dance. It's not like she has anything else going on. Still—she is a part of our family and I do love that beautiful, carrot-eating girl. If only she could learn to excuse herself *before* passing gas, we'd all be living better. It's just rude and so unattractive for a lady of her stature. Buffy remains something of a mystery to me. *Arf! It's a bird, Buffy! Get it girl!* She loves chasing birds. I think they make her feel young again.

Betty Boop is a ten-year-old "Designer Breed" (aka "Mutt") and the linearly-challenged pup in the group. Such a silly, little, scrappy thing. We sometimes call her "BoopBoopDiBoop" as she starts walking around in circles. Crazy kid. Oh, and she loves peanut butter. I guess we all do; I just find it hard to talk with a mouthful. Either way, Betty Boop rarely disrupts my routine, so that's cool.

Carla Mae is a nine-year-old Lhasa Apso and a great example of how different Lhasa Apsos can be. She grew up as a "biter" and arrived here that way. That was one challenge. My other challenge with this little tomboy was her inability to cut loose and play a little. She doesn't seem to have that need to bite anymore, unless you get between her and her food. And while teaching someone how to play and dance and have fun isn't easy, I am an inspired and enthusiastic teacher. One of my proudest accomplishments in this area was teaching Carla Mae to dance. She never really got my strut down pat, but she has a style and a wiggle all her own.

You go sister! Dancin' dancin' dancin'! Watch her get down, watch her get down… ba da do do do do do dancin' machine!

Then, there's the human. Cute (though she could stand to be a bit furrier), fun (when she stays focused on the moment), and fairly fit. She can be a bit slow to get moving, but does pretty well keeping up overall. Most importantly, she brings home doggy treats. *Doggy Treats! Woof! Wake up, everyone! It's time for doggy treats!* Bow-*wow*, those are the best.

Where was I? Human… blah, blah, blah. Oh yeah: What's-her-face. Despite the fact that she brings home doggy treats, she's certifiably crazy. No, I don't mean the "oh you're so crazy fun" crazy. She's got delusions of grandeur, this one. On some level, it's as if she thinks she's in charge. It might be a little cute at times, but for the most part it's terribly frustrating. I may not be a psychiatrist in real life, but I did play one on TV. Ha! Just joking. That's me. I like to use comedy whenever possible. But in all seriousness: C-R-A-Z-Y.

One time the human had new bedroom furniture delivered. WOOF! I watched those delivery clowns take things out and move things and bring more things in. After they left I had to spend *hours* wrestling everything into place perfectly, breaking all the pieces in—chewing up and adequately marking the headboard, frame, night stands, dresser, chest of drawers—the whole kit 'n caboodle. At times, I had to hang upside down to get a good chomp in. When the human came in, I was just finishing up my spectacular work on the bed frame and she made the oddest screeching sound of approbation. Then, before I can take my richly deserved pats-n-kudos, she breaks out the water gun in some kind of deranged effort to reprimand me. I later discovered this odd screech to be a noise of dismay, often followed by *"Dammit Goo!"* Evidently the human wanted to break everything in herself. I frankly don't think she has the teeth for it, much less the physical agility. Can you say "control freak?" Still—a little appreciation wouldn't have been out of line. It's times like this that I just have to think about the doggy treats. WOOOOF!! Doggy treats…

Then there was the time that Carla Mae bit her, so the human went and put on a helmet, gloves, and all of her motorcycle gear. To ride a motorcycle? Nope. She did it to pick up Carla Mae and get bitten again. I just shake my head and wonder, "How in the world is that better than a motorcycle ride?" Then the human kept saying, "No Carla Mae. What you really want is *attention*." I was there. What Carla Mae really wanted was to bite her and when the human came back with that ridiculous outfit on, it freaked Carla Mae out and she wanted to bite her again. Finally Carla Mae gave in to the crazy woman and fell asleep in her arms. For whatever crazy reason, they both seemed happier after that night and we were all able to get back on my expertly master-minded schedule (designed specifically to support the needs of one Alpha Dog Extraordinaire).

Once again, things are getting a little out of sync around here (due to my work on *my* book). The human convinced me to let her "help out with marketing the book" and now suddenly she thinks she's a writer and wants to add chapters of her own to – get this – "clarify things." Yeah, wonderful. Let's let the crazy woman "clarify" it all for us. The nightmare part of this whole journey is that I'm a little short on cash and really need the human's financial contributions. So I don't have a boat-load of choices.

I need to let her think she has *some* kind of say in what's going on. Just know that if this book ends up being titled anything other than "MaGoo the Great: Cute, Fearless, and Ready for Action," I *will* eat the human's favorite pair of kick-boxing shoes. Then I'll blame it on Buffy (whose gas makes you wonder if she has been eating gym shoes anyway) or on Carla Mae (feisty little biter she can be).

All human frailties aside, I do love that frenzied, little blockhead with all my heart and all the bones I've ever buried. I'll never forget my first day on the job. She picked me up in the niftiest car ever (there was no roof!), and smiled and chatted ceaselessly all the way home. I took it all in – playing the role of interested observer. *Cool car. Whoa! What was that? Did you see that dog? Hey – scope out the back seat. Check out the front seat. Tree! Did you see the tree? Hey – what's this under the seat? A French fry! Yes! Yummmm. RRUFF! The human's face tastes better than the French fry. Is that another car? Whoa – a truck! Wonder what the human's fur tastes like. Kind of flowery if you ask me. Is that something in her ear? BIRDS! BIRDS! There must be a million birds! Can I see what's in the glove box? Why are we stopping? Oh – now we're moving again. Can we go in that store? No! Never mind. There are little humans in there. Oh my, it's a cat! I swear – a cat! Just walking down the street. Imagine that. And another tree! Wow – it looks like there is a fire hydrant on every corner. And a lake!! Oh – I could get used to this.*

It was a day of sunshine and love, French fries and fire hydrants. And new beginnings. Little did I know the challenges I would be faced with down the road. Little did I know the joy I would come to know leading a family of beautiful misfits. I'd trade all the doggy treats in the world (okay, maybe not "all" but *most* of them, anyway) to continue to provide for and protect my crazy family. We have BIG fun and with me around – there's never a dull moment.

ARRRF! ARF! ARF! Sparky! For real? Keep it moving! WOOF! Don't even think about being rude! WOOF! WOOF! Yep. Keep those paws moving buddy. No need for you to be marking territory 'round these parts.

It's a never-ending job, I tell ya.

Chapter Two

A Girl and Her Dog

As we begin, barely scratching the surface of this project, several concerns occur to me. First, I'm writing a book with a dog (who honestly believes he's in charge). Second, Mr. MaGoo has a flair for the dramatic and views "facts" as something one can take or leave. Example: while I did gear up in motorcycle attire to hold Carla Mae, I left the helmet behind, making use only of the gloves and leather jacket. Much more on that story later. And, for the record, I was upset that the little bugger chewed up my new furniture, *not* because I wanted to chew it up myself. Third, Mr. MaGoo has gnawed through two keyboards, one mouse, and a can of sunflower seeds I had kept on my desk. Already my financial responsibility has become greater than anticipated.

My final concern is that my friends and family are ready to have me committed.

I'm Kelly Preston. The "human" and current "provider of goods and services" to four high-need dogs.

My love of animals started early. I was raised in the town of Brogue, Pennsylvania, a tiny hamlet in a rural area outside of Red Lion, Pennsylvania which is itself a rural area outside of York, Pennsylvania, which is itself a rural area in the south-central part of the state. Along with its sister city of Lancaster, York is known for its farmland and its population of Pennsylvania Dutch. Not that there isn't some industry there, as well, but I don't remember seeing much of that anywhere around Brogue.

Our ten-acre family property was nestled snugly within a community of working farms. Dad was a school teacher and Mom was a stay-at-home mom taking care of the house, me, my younger sister Colleen, and my younger brother Shawn, though not necessarily in that order. Shawn was born with Down's syndrome, a congenital disorder resulting in mental retardation. Shawn required a lot of attention. But he was a true angel and everybody's favorite. He was innocent and loving and had a wonderful sense of humor, always smiling, always laughing. Shawn loved life in a way that I don't think most people ever do.

I was six when Shawn came home from the hospital. I don't remember exactly when I discovered he was different. I remember when Shawn was just a toddler he developed a serious infection that had him in the hospital's intensive care unit, and had my parents worried and anxious in ways I had never seen before. It scared me. But Shawn made it back home and all was right again. As I got older, I began to learn more about his condition. I learned how different Shawn was and that he would always be different. But Colleen and I treated him like anybody else, Colleen especially, always treating him with her older sister style of tough love.

We were one of the few families around not actually living on a working farm. Although I had dogs and pet bunnies, all my girlfriends had horses, cows, pigs, and chickens. It was the horses that made me most envious. I wanted one desperately, and I voiced my desire to my dad. A lot. All the time, in fact. "Horses are a lot of work," he would say, and the conversation would end.

Then one Christmas morning when I was eleven, I was delighted to walk downstairs and see nothing less than a saddle sitting under the tree with a big red bow on it. It could mean only one thing. I ran out of the house looking for the horse that I was certain Dad had finally bought for me. I looked all over – front yard, back yard, side yard, garage. Then Dad came out after me.

"The saddle is a promise, Kelly. If you promise you'll take care of the horse, promise to be completely responsible for it, we'll get one."

"When?" I cried.

"After the barn."

"What barn?" I blinked back at him.

"The barn you're going to help me build for the horse." And so when spring came along and the weather warmed up and the ground thawed, Dad and I went to work building a barn, something Mom had some serious reservations about. "She's eleven years old!" I would hear her telling Dad, but there I was, mixing cement, hammering boards, laying bricks. I lost a couple fingernails along the way, but by the end of that summer, we had ourselves a barn. Soon after that, I had myself a horse. In fact, we ended up acquiring two horses because Colleen – a typical middle child who was smart enough to let her older sister be the one to eventually wear Dad down (as well as spend her summer building a barn!) – suddenly decided she'd like to have a horse, too.

Without a lot of knowledge about horses, we got lucky on one and unlucky on another. Colleen's horse, Honey, was sweet and gentle; the perfect horse for new owners. My horse, Silver Boy, was a dapple gray horse, the kind I had often seen being ridden through the corner of our property on fox hunts, the kind I had always wanted. Unfortunately we found out pretty quickly that Silver Boy wasn't about to allow anybody to ride him. What we didn't know when we bought him was that he hadn't been trained for riding. Silver Boy was an Amish plow horse.

We sold Silver Boy and Colleen and I shared Honey for a little while, but I wanted a horse of my own (it was me who built the barn, after all) and Dad was good enough to surprise me one day with Danny Boy, a registered quarter horse. I grew up with Danny Boy. We fox hunted and studied dressage together. He was my friend and confidant, and we rode everywhere. Danny Boy gave me confidence in myself. He was a challenging horse, much more so than the gentle Honey. He was always pushing the boundaries and needing to be reined in. Having to meet these challenges helped build my self-esteem and bring me out of the adolescent shell I'd been in.

Colleen realized fairly early in the game that caring for horses was a lot more than she had the heart and passion for. She threw herself into sports, mostly track and field, basketball, and field hockey, while I threw myself into my horses, now two of them.

I loved Danny Boy profoundly, but sadly his life was to end with the gradual onset of navicular syndrome, a hoof disease that rendered him unable to even walk at the end. Gratefully, I still had Honey, with whom I had won my first two blue ribbons.

She was versatile and intelligent and adapted easily to different riding styles. We shared good times and were the best of hunting and jumping buddies. Shawn loved Honey, too. We'd put Shawn up on Honey who would ride him around the yard, Shawn beaming the whole time. It got me involved with a local therapeutic riding program for the disabled and those with special needs, which was wonderfully rewarding for me.

After Colleen and I left home for college, our parents sold Honey to a neighboring family who had a son with cerebral palsy. Bradley, their son, loved Honey and she patiently accepted and seemed to understand his difficulty controlling voluntary muscles. She had had, after all, significant experience with a disabled child in Shawn. Plus, I had given riding lessons to the family and they already knew and loved Honey. She was a perfect fit for their family. She lived out her final years on their lovely farm.

Though my horse years were behind me, little did I know what was in store for me pet-wise. Sharing a home with the motley group of canines I now possess is the result of an unpredictable series of events that all began one day shortly after I had graduated from college.

I had opened an aerobics studio in York. One afternoon, walking home from the studio, I spotted the cutest Lhasa Apso puppy in a pet shop window. I don't know what made me stop, but I couldn't seem to take my eyes off of her. Though I had no business thinking about getting a dog, what with the demands of my business, all I could think of later that night was the puppy in the window. I decided that if she was still there the next day, she was meant to be mine.

I rose early the next morning, bolting out of bed, wanting to waste no time getting to the pet store. Somewhere in the course of the night I had already fallen in love with this little puppy and the idea of her going home with someone else made my heart ache. I raced to the small shop on Main Street, stopping short at the now-empty window where the Lhasa Apso had appeared the day before. My heart sank. Then, before I could recover from my disappointment, she jumped up, paws on the window, wagging her little tail. I purchased her on the spot and called friends and family to let them know about the new addition to my household.

Gizmo, as I named her, became my constant companion and the aerobics studio's official mascot. She ran on the hardwood floors and enjoyed chasing her favorite toys across the smooth, suspended surface.

After the studio closed, I accepted a job in the Washington, D.C. metropolitan area, and Gizmo and I moved to Northern Virginia. We went everywhere together: boating, sailing, horseback riding, lunches at Mickey D's. Gizmo modeled and even appeared in an art show. We had simultaneous beauty/pamper appointments and enjoyed the sights and sounds of D.C.

We saw hard times in D.C. too. One otherwise meaningless Tuesday night, I returned home after teaching an aerobics class, stopping at my front door, momentarily baffled by the fact that the deadbolt was in place, along with the chain, two things that could only be accessed from the *inside* of the door. How strange, I thought to myself. I don't remember doing that. And how could I do it anyway? Then it dawned on me: somebody else had to have done it. Somebody had entered my apartment.

With no thought at all that perhaps the burglar might still be on the premises, I rushed around the back, running in through the back door with only one thing on my mind: *where's Gizmo?!* Had they hurt her, or worse? I looked everywhere. Our peaceful dwelling had been ransacked. I searched frantically, under the bed, behind the sofa, in the closets. Finally, rushing past the bathroom I heard a whimpering. I burst in and swept the shower curtain aside and there was my Gizmo, cowering and shaking in the tub. I held her and comforted her and let her know that everything was going to be all right.

Gizmo did the same for me on more than one occasion. There were bad relationships, even one particularly abusive one. Abusive relationships start out gradually. The abuser sucks you in with charm, or good looks, or both. A low sense of self-esteem quickens the process. This particular abuser was especially good at it, making me so dependent on the relationship that I quickly forgave the initial demands and controlling behavior. But of course it got worse, as such relationships always do, and the controlling behavior grew into abuse. It took all my strength to break away from him, but for my own sanity I knew that I needed to do so. On the night I finally ended it, a night of screaming and threats from my now ex-boyfriend, I eventually found myself back home, alone, except for Gizmo, who jumped into my lap as I sat crying on the bed and stayed with me all night, letting me hold her as I rocked back and forth, my tears dampening her fur.

She did the same thing the night my parents called and told me that Shawn had passed away. It was strange – I suppose I knew on some level that Shawn wasn't going to live forever, yet, me being the eldest; I somehow thought he would outlive me. My denial of the inevitability of his condition made the news that much more of a shock, and I was devastated. I thought of his smiling face sitting atop Honey and I couldn't stop crying. Gizmo never left my side that night, either.

In July 2000, my company was bought out and in October that same year, I was transferred to California to help with the company's website migration. Gizmo and I loaded up all of our worldly possessions and with Gizmo's blanket and favorite toy beside her, off we went on yet another adventure.

Fortunately, Gizmo loved road trips. I told everyone that she was my co-pilot. She would stand and watch through the window. In my convertible with the top down, Gizmo would enjoy standing up on the rear seat, looking out the back. Despite the day trips and pamper parties, life in the D.C. metropolitan area had been a troubled one for me, yet it was still relatively close to home, just an hour away from Brogue. Now I was really moving away. But Gizmo was coming with me! We were headed west to a new home – but to what would ultimately be the beginning of the end.

Shortly after arriving in California, I noticed Gizmo developing an unusual and persistent head tilt. I watched her more closely than ever and after a couple days passed with no change, I grabbed the local phone book and found a nearby vet. Dr. Keith Hilinski and his staff at Rolling Hills Veterinary Hospital were understanding and kind, even setting aside office rules to accept my out-of-state check. Dr. Hilinski remains my veterinarian to this day.

A roller coaster of events finally led up to the ordering of MRIs and the tests confirmed our worst suspicions. Gizmo had a brain tumor.

The neurologist informed me the tumor was located at the base of the brain stem and was almost impossible to access. There was a chance that surgery could be fatal or she could be paralyzed for life. Radiation therapy would have required a biopsy and again, would be almost impossible to get to. If I chose to let nature take its course, I would have maybe two weeks to be with her.

My heart would not stop breaking and my phone bill soared as I reached out to family and friends. My father, understanding my pain, tried, in typical male fashion, to "solve" my problem.

"Kelly," he said, "I do hope that when Gizmo dies you don't waste any time in getting another dog." I was speechless. As if dogs were interchangeable. I knew on some level that he meant well. He understood that I was not one to be alone for long. I had had an animal of some description to love and care for my whole life. In retrospect, the walk past the pet shop's window to discover Gizmo that day was inevitable. Though nothing could replace Gizmo, Dad knew me well. He knew I needed something at least to help fill the void.

It was the right thing for him to advise. But it was the wrong time. I wanted understanding and sympathy for what I was going through. I needed someone to listen. It was far too soon to be talking about getting another dog. Yet two weeks later, it would turn out that that's exactly what I would be doing. Yep, Dad knew me well. But if he only knew then what "getting another dog" would eventually lead to!

I decided against the precarious surgery and procedures and promised Gizmo I would not allow her to suffer pain or lose her dignity. If all we had together was two weeks, we'd simply have to make the most of it. After all, I told myself, sometimes less time means more quality time.

Dr. Hilinski had cautioned me that Gizmo was likely to have sensitivity to light. "She may prefer a dark room, due to potential headaches," he explained. I got to thinking about Gizmo and sunlight, and how I feel with migraines. A dark room was easy enough while we were home, but Gizmo loved to go places. And places we would go! So we went shopping and I found Gizmo an adorable hat to perfectly shade her eyes. All the way home, Gizmo stood up against the car window. She was my co-pilot again. People along the way would look and smile at this sweet dog in her cute hat. Gizmo seemed happy and comfortable.

That weekend, Gizmo's spirit was revived. She played with her toys again and seemed like her old self. During the weekend I tried to put myself in Gizmo's place. I wondered what I would want to do if I had only two weeks to live. I made a list, and over the course of the next couple of weeks we started checking off the items. We visited the California canyons. We explored lakes and mountains and apple orchards. We traveled to see the seals at La Jolla. Everywhere we went during those final days; Gizmo rode with her hat on.

One day we went to a leash-free dog beach. Gizmo had never been on a beach in her life. She proceeded cautiously at first through the sand, not at all sure what to make of the new sensation on her paws, but in no time she was running, running like a playful puppy. She'd run towards the water and come to a grinding halt where the sand was wet and bark at the crashing waves as they cascaded towards her. When they kept coming and she finally realized she was not going to be successful in bullying them back into the ocean, she turned and decided to run some more on the powder dry sand of the beach. Eventually she tired and came to me and we sat down together and looked out at the water. We probably sat like that for an hour or more, and then Gizmo looked up into my face as if to say she was ready to go home.

Fortunately I was blessed to work with a company that allowed me some flexibility in my schedule. Understanding and compassionate, they allowed me to spend time with Gizmo as if she was my child which, in a way, she was.

While caring for Gizmo, I constantly scanned the Internet for nutritional information and new research about her condition. During one late night session, I came across an Anaheim animal shelter's web page advertising a cute mutt with the adorable name of Betty Boop. I called and inquired about her, expressing some interest, but really more curious at that point than anything. I thanked them for their time and temporarily put the matter out of my mind. But it wasn't long before the shelter called back telling me that Betty Boop was mine for the taking. So, in the car I went for the two-hour drive to Anaheim.

As I was filling out the paperwork for Betty Boop, I noticed a four-year old Cocker Spaniel that had been brought in that same day. She had been rescued from an abusive home, hair so snarled that her front legs were matted together and she could barely walk. Then one of the staff members brought out Betty Boop and my heart fell hard for her. She was too cute for words. But, just like Gizmo, she was a special-needs dog. Betty Boop had apparent developmental problems. She wasn't eating or drinking, and could only walk in a tight circle. She was sad, but she was beautiful. The people at the shelter felt as if she would outgrow her problems if cared for properly. I wanted to take her right home.

First I had to ask about the little Cocker they had brought in. The woman in front of me had already adopted her, I was told, and it made me happy to think the tragic-looking puppy had found a home. But before Betty Boop and I could finish saying our hello's to each other, it was decided the woman ahead of me, being a frequent business traveler, was not going to be able to commit to the care that the little Cocker Spaniel was going to require. So what could I do? I left the shelter that day with *two* dogs. Both of whom would require special attention and a lot of love.

At home, the three girls – Gizmo, Betty Boop, and Buffy (as I named the Cocker) – bonded instantly. We were now a happy family of four. Of course, Mr. MaGoo and Carla Mae came along later.

Gizmo's condition gradually deteriorated. Seizures became more frequent and more intense. During the last seizure Gizmo whined out in pain and I found myself thinking sadly, "Today's the day." We had spent eleven years together, Gizmo and I. I had promised her I would not allow her to suffer and so her sorrowful cry led me to Dr. Hilinski's office once again where he gave me the options. He could provide pain medication and I could take Gizmo home. Just for me to bring her back in a couple more days? I thought there's a point in time when one is no longer prolonging life, but rather procrastinating death. I was given a prognosis from the neurologist of two weeks with Gizmo. We had received six months. Now came the time to be strong, the time to have faith. I took the other option and signed consent to euthanize my beautiful and faithful companion and to mercifully put an end to her unnecessary suffering.

The doctor administered the shot and I sat with Gizmo, looking into her eyes. Life was fading from them and she appeared tired and spent. But then she surprisingly perked up, mustering some strength from somewhere. It was as if she wasn't quite ready to leave, and I began to sense why. Gizmo was more than a friend. She thought of herself as my protector, my confidant. She didn't want to leave me alone. "But Mommy will be all right," I whispered in her ear. She seemed to relax at this. "It's okay to go," I said, tears welling in my eyes. "I don't want you in any more pain, Gizmo." With that, she put her head down and breathed a final sigh. My Gizmo was gone.

Gizmo prepared me for much of what was to come – a journey that would include coping with Betty Boop's neurological issues, Buffy's fears, Carla Mae's challenges, and Mr. MaGoo's daily demands. A journey within that would help me discover devotion, patience, leadership, and unconditional love.

The current members of the household take up a lot of time and energy, but I still think of Gizmo. She's never really left me and I'm reminded of her often, seeing her in some way in the faces of the other dogs, remembering her running on the beach, and wearing that adorable hat which sits faithfully even now on a shelf in my bedroom – the hat that once adorned the head of my confidant, teacher, and best friend.

Chapter Three

MaGoo Reels the Crazy Lady Back In

What in the world was *that*? Who is "Gizmo" and correct me if I'm wrong, but wouldn't she belong in a book entitled "*Other* Dogs"? *Whoa.* And horses—really? I fail to see how horses have anything to do with any of this. It would be amazingly awesome if the crazy human could stick to the game plan and write about me. I am, after all, the reason why every one of you picked up this book. If you wanted to read about farms and bunnies and horses, I'm guessing you would've picked up something else. *Can I get an AMEN?*

There are fifty-seven words and phrases in the English language relating to being bored and every one of them crossed my mind while reading Chapter Two: afflict, annoy, be boring, bend one's ear, bored to death, bored sick, bored beyond belief, blah, burned out, common, cause weariness, destroyer of delight, disinterest, doomsday parade, drab, dry, energy-sucking, exhausting, flat, hibernating ha ha, ho-hum, hypnagogic, inactive, inert, irk, irritate, jade, jacked up, lackluster, lame-o, monotonous, mundane, murderer of merriment, nap-inducing, O'Doul's buzz, out of it, ordinary, pedestrian, platitudinous, plebeian, poke-in-the-eye pleasure, predictable, relief of joy, Rip Van Winkle reception, sleeper spree, shoot me please someone shoot me, somnolent, snooze fest, tire, trite, turn off, unimaginative, uninspired, vanilla, wear out, weary, wish you'd stop talking, yawn party.

WOOF! Come on humanoid. Get with the program. Stop being so self-centered and think about what's important here—me. Although in all fairness, I really liked the parts about Shawn. Didn't you? He sounds like a happy-go-lucky kind of guy. I think we could be close friends. I'd love to have someone around who was always smiling and happy and recognizing the wonder of each day. Oh sure, he might be too much sunshine for the grouchy ones out there, but he'd be *perfect* for me to hang out with.

Still—(minus the Shawn parts) I think we'd *all* rather go back and count to see if there are really fifty-seven phrases describing reader response than be forced to unravel that mess again. I would pay top dollar to get the hour back I invested in going through Chapter Two. Once again, it looks like I'll be the straw stirring *this* drink.

Speaking of "top dollar," I am reminded of the day the human made her single largest, unparalleled, and most memorable monetary investment of her entire life.

The pet shop was wild with the sights, sounds, and smells of a magical medley of animal absurdities—dogs, cats, birds, snakes, mice, fish, lizards. Perfect pandemonium; a brouhaha brunch, if you will. I was, of course, in charge of the grand phantasmagoria.

The human walked in and just like all the ones before her, fell in love with me instantly. Pecuniary arrangements were discussed and the purchase was made. I was happy and excited. Pet shop life had been good to me, but it was a huge responsibility sitting there looking adorable all day (not that it didn't come naturally) and I looked forward to something a little less demanding. Yep—I was young and naïve and completely oblivious to futuristic matters. I quickly glanced at the human's receipt and saw a "1" and a "5" and a lot of zeros. That could only mean one thing: the human dropped 1.5 million dollars on yours truly. (At least I think so...I didn't really *count* the zeroes.) It seemed a *bit* pricey, but I had *no* idea what lay ahead of me. The price paid probably should have been my first clue. *Woof.*

The ride home was a frenzy of fragrances and views and tastes to be savored. The air was crisp with anticipation, the sun bright with possibilities. We arrived at the house and the human muttered something about "meeting the others." I was way too busy scoping out the neighborhood and all the lawns and fire hydrants to pay much attention.

Upon entering the dwelling I was greeted by a lovely Cocker Spaniel named Buffy. She was gracious and kind. I was grateful to see that there was a canine lady of the house and I wasn't going to be stuck with strictly human training and protection as my primary job description. Don't get me wrong—I love humans! Well—*most* of them anyway. It's just always nice to have another dog in the pack. And Buffy was entirely lovely. I felt welcomed instantly.

I then noticed a timid little mutt in the corner sleeping. I heard the human say, "This is Betty Boop." Too funny; I knew a bird at the pet shop named "Betty Boop." But this shy, tiny animal was no squawking, screeching maniac like that bird. I sensed the dog's apprehension and gingerly approached her. I nuzzled in close and whispered, "It's okay. There's a new sheriff in town. I'll take care of you." I felt her anxiety fade and her spirit lift. I have that effect on others. It's a gift.

I was there for Betty Boop when the human brought her home from the doctor's office only weeks later. I'm not comfortable when Betty Boop is out of my sight and in the human's sole care. However, I have little choice but to trust Betty Boop's professional medical care to the human. It's not like the human is going to let me drive her car. I have a hard enough time getting her to share the household computer. Sometimes letting go is the hardest thing of all.

I realized almost immediately that my single, greatest challenge would be the human. I set out to complete a few simple tests. She seemed to enjoy peek-a-boo and since she grasped the concept with a fair amount of ease, I attempted to teach her peek-a-*poo*. Well, that one didn't go over nearly as well, so I decided to focus my energies on a comprehensive evaluation of the habitat security instead, and resolved to come back to project "lighten up human" at a later date or perhaps intermittingly as time permitted.

Several glaring security issues were apparent, primarily involving the lack of boundaries being maintained to keep others out. I struggled to inform the human of the gravitas of the situation; she resisted badly and I, with no alternative, finally masterminded the perfect plot to illustrate the dilemma. I deduced the best way to *tell* her was to *show* her how easily one could get out—because if one can get *out*, one can most certainly get *in*. Yep—Security 101.

I opted for a simple patio escape. The neighbors always seemed nice and while I was out maybe I would stop by and say hello.

Watching, waiting... okay go! Up, over, down, under, around the corner—between the bushes, by a tree... I was free! *The grass felt cool and cushioned my every pounce. Sweet, reckless abandon!*

Within minutes, I was greeting the neighbors with sheer exuberance. Of course, they were perfectly thrilled to make my acquaintance. Then as the full impact of this security breach hit her, the human's screams of utter panic echoed throughout the land. When I arrived back at her side to explain this was only a demonstration, she held me close and sobbed tears of gratitude. She finally realized my true worth as a protector and accomplished security professional.

From that moment on, things changed between us. The human seemed more interested and expressed gratitude more freely. Peek-a-*poo* never really caught on, so I ended up letting that one go.

To this very day, I continue to maintain a close watch on the entire household—especially the shifty human. I feign interest in her chores and pretend to help out with trivial tasks. When emotions rise or when I feel like I need to be entertained, I provide levity and amusement. It's truly a wonder these guys ever survived without me.

Yawn. I've earned a nap today and just in time as it looks like the human is ready to butt in. Y'all might want to save this next chapter for a sleepless night—it is bound to be a cure.

Chapter Four

MaGoo Maintains Control!

WAHOOOOO!! I'm a dog writer, I'm a dog writer. Writing up a storm. I am loving life today! The human had to go out of town on business (whatever *that* means) and we are home alone with the sitter. *Home alone, Home-a-lone! Life is good; we're home alone!!!*

And, get this, because the dog sitter is here—I have a personal assistant today. I told her all about my book and she was *amazed.* I also told her that I required doggy treats every hour on the hour. Such a beautiful, naïve thing. Though admittedly she is quite kind and loving and does everything in her power to please me *and* help care for my sisters. Whatever the human is paying her, I'm sure it's not enough.

What are "business trips" and why does the human take them? Where does she go? Why can't she do her business right here like the rest of us? How long will she be gone? How much writing can I get done in the interim? When the human's away, the dogs shall play!

Well kids—might as well get down to the matter at hand. I have the human's notes right here in front me. She was planning on using this chapter to tell you all about Betty Boop. As if *she* could possibly know more about Betty Boop than I do! Please. I've skimmed through the whole shebang and I don't see a lot of worthwhile material. So—I'm pitching her impressions and starting from scratch. You can thank me later.

The human found Betty Boop in a shelter. I was still working at the pet shop when both Betty Boop and Buffy were adopted. I've heard the story a million times. The human drove to Anaheim—a mystical place founded by Germans in 1857. It was a big experiment in communal living back in the day—with dogs, *naturally*, being the focal point. Tourists consistently flocked to the region with profound interest. Disney even set up camp in the area to take care of some of the overflow. They created several dog characters as a way of thanking the dogs for their obvious contribution to the company's huge success. Today, Anaheim remains a canine collective. There's like a big shelter and activists and dog parks and groomers and stuff. If there's one region that has their priorities straight, it's Anaheim—where dogs rule and humans drool.

When I first met Betty Boop, I remember thinking how she seemed rather chewed up and spit out—not just in regards to her health, but to her spirit as well. My guess is that her life prior to living with the human had been no bed of roses, nor endless supply of doggie treats.

Hang on a second kids, looks like we have a perimeter intrusion in progress! I can't believe this!

Woof! Sparky! Grrrrrr… Arf! Arf! Back it up blockhead! I'm in the middle of writing a book! Have some respect. Yep—just move on down the road little doggy. Let your human lead the way you mangy little mutt. I have deadlines, an editor with an attitude, and no time for the likes of you. Loooooo-ser.

I probably shouldn't be so hard on Sparky. In all fairness, I did kind of start off on the wrong paw with him. I was new in the hood and when Sparky and his human approached, *my* human said, "Hi, Jerry." So I laughed out loud and mocked the dog: "Hi, I'm Jerry," I teased mercilessly in a stupid voice. What a dumb name for a dog, right? Yeah, ummmm… that was Sparky's *human's* name. Sparky snapped at me and then whimpered pathetically away.

So now our relationship is strained, to say the least. Sparky is an insufferable, passive-aggressive personality disordered dog. He's the type that smiles to your face and acts like everything is cool, then as soon as he thinks you aren't watching—*boom!* He's marking territory in *my* yard. Two-faced total loser. He should get over it. It was an honest mistake and "Jerry" *is* a stupid name for a dog. Some dogs are way too sensitive for their own good. Big sissy mutt.

Anyway, back to sweet, little BoopBoopDiBoop. Betty Boop was born with "water-on-the-brain" or Hydrocephalus (I totally just Googled that). Poor little Booper! I just always thought she was silly and possibly allergic to the vet. She flat-lined there one time. It was crazy. I watched my beautiful human turn pale. I think this is how humans look when they're scared and their hearts are breaking. But Betty Boop pulled through for us. She's tougher than she looks. Or she's part cat and has more than one life.

Another time, Betty Boop had a different kind of allergic reaction to the vet. The human went out of town and had left us there for a few days. Betty Boop didn't eat the food they gave her (did I mention she was picky?) and refused to drink their water (probably not the bottled water our princess is accustomed to). By the time the human returned, Betty Boop's tongue was like sandpaper and she ended up with a respiratory infection. That's an infection that affects your breathing parts. It was yet more meds for the little girl. It's a wonder she has room for them all. Booper's so dainty, and almost completely blind. I'm sure it was a terrifying ordeal for her.

I've always sensed her vulnerability and have accordingly stepped up to the plate as the very "ne plus ultra" of patience and protection. A lesser dog might sense the same frailty and seek to eliminate or bring harm to Betty Boop. Mark my words—I will *never* let that happen to my sweet, little sister. She loves freely and expresses gratitude easily. She is an angel and deserves the respect and care of such. There's something magical about a dog with more than one life.

Betty Boop is a high-maintenance pup, though. The human gives her medicines at regular intervals throughout the day and Betty Boop seems to take *forever* to finish a meal—like 30 and 45 minutes sometimes. Sometimes the human has to sit with her, encouraging her to eat. Plus Betty Boop only eats one certain kind of dog food and snacks primarily on peanut butter. Not me! I like to eat *anything* that doesn't eat me first—no encouragement needed. I'm really fast, too. I could probably eat this whole house in the time it takes Betty Boop to tackle a single bowl of kibble. And Betty Boop *only* drinks bottled water. It seems to me, she's missing a lot of liquid oomph experience if all she drinks is freaking bottled water. She can't possibly know all that she's missing. But, some of us live the drama, while others just sit back and enjoy the show. And little sister definitely enjoys the show! She is the president of my fan club. Ask her—she *loves* me. No other pup is quite so generous with her love and attention. She never tires of my jokes or grows weary of my antics. Betty Boop is my indefatigable audience… until she eats. What a buzz kill.

After eating, Betty Boop is out like a light. I think she sleeps best when being held by the human (which is often). Those two just can't seem to get enough of all the fluffy foo-foo/lovey dovey crap. Girls. What's a guy to do? They're so goofy. I try to keep it light, while maintaining the structure of a well-planned schedule. Let the girls do all the kissy-faced foolishness; they're good at it. And it *is* cute to watch.

Speaking of cute and who is *not…*

Woof! Yo King Ignoramus! Leave that little dog alone! You big bully—I'll rip you to shreds. Woof!

That's King. He's a big stupid German Shepherd in our neighborhood. No matter how hard I try, I just can't like that dog. He's mean and ugly and he has scared the crap out of my sisters on more than one occasion. I'll tell you guys more about him later. Back to the Boopster…

Sometimes the water in Betty Boop's brain makes her shake almost violently. Maybe she's just trying to shake some of it out. The human calls these episodes "seizures," which is ridiculous—like what is she seizing? Is she abducting someone? Are these the actions of a dog commandeering a vehicle? Is she apprehending, arresting, confiscating, grabbing, pinching, or snatching something? Perhaps she's just s*eizing* the moment? I don't think so. Note to human: Dictionary.com called. They said give 'em a try sometime.

Often, the human walks with Betty Boop in the house—staying by her side, encouraging her to walk a straight line. It doesn't look like that's really going to happen on its own. But BoopBoopDiBoop is a trooper and if anyone knows the power of a positive mental attitude, it's her.

Doctors never expected Betty Boop to live past six months. She's ten years old now. Doctors are stupid sometimes. But then again, they didn't know Betty Boop had Mr. MaGoo and the human on her team. Together, nothing bad will ever happen to this adorable angel. I am "MaGoo the Protector," after all. And the human could win awards for being the single most fluffy foo-foo, dog-loving human ever. As if she doesn't have enough to take care of already, she runs all over town conspicuously looking for dogs that need rescued. More often than not, it's a night or two till the strays find a family to call their own. We've all been in tough, transitional situations—it's scary, it's uncertain. My sisters and I try to keep everything low-key, so as not to startle our guests. While they may not find a home with an alpha dog as rocking awesome as me, there must be a bajillion dog-loving humans out there, right? Maybe one of those lucky dogs will end up running their own pack one day. They say there's an alpha dog in all of us just barking to get out.

And ironically there's Sparky again kids—being led by his human Jerry. The madness never ends.

Woof! Seems you're the exception to that rule Sparky! You wouldn't know how to step up to the plate and be an alpha dog if your dog chow depended on it. Weenie.

Where was I? Oh yes… in many ways, watching the human care for and love us so deeply, has taught me to be more loving and sensitive. Betty Boop taught the human and the human has taught me—dude, it's like the *circle of love*. Without Betty Boop really *needing* that very special kind of love and patience, I frankly don't know that the human would have gotten to this level on her own. And without having seen for myself the human in action, I may have stayed entirely focused on the security and entertainment aspects of my awesomely lofty position here—completely without regard to frivolous things like "patience". But I do see that such a thing does have a place in a family.

That's patience in a family, Sparky. Do you hear me? I have no patience for trespassers and lame-o dogs like you. You better believe I'm writing all of this down. WOOF!

The human has the patience of a saint. I don't care how crazy things get around here, when she realizes a canine need exists—treats for me, a hug for Betty Boop, a kiss from Buffy, special attention for Carla Mae, or a car ride for a stray, she jumps to take care of us. Okay, *sometimes* she jumps faster than other times, but really, she is entirely adequate—for a human. And it all started with Betty Boop. She prepared the human well for what was to come. Little BoopBoopDiBoop.

Bow-wow. I've been writing like a dog all day. Think I'll go hit up the sitter for another treat and then hit the hay for a bit. Wake me if the human shows up. It's my job to jump all over her when she walks in.

Chapter Five

360 Degrees of Protection

Let me commence by saying that clowns (by the canine definition) should *not* be allowed to own dogs. You humans have rules and regulations about everything from baloney to bubble gum. Why not regulate this? Come up with a test and when the clown doesn't pass you can say, "You suck at being a member of the human species, therefore you cannot own a dog." It would all be so simple then. *Easy-peasy cheddar cheesy.* But oh no—let's have 500 million more conversations about "the economy." That'll make a difference. Humans' priorities are completely out of whack.

Alas, there *are* clowns who own dogs, dogs that, *if they're lucky*, will end up in a shelter somewhere far away from the human that left a "funny" taste in their mouth to begin with. Buffy had that kind of luck. Her owner was a total blockhead, loser-face clown (blatant, unbridled harshness intended). It makes me so angry; I want to chew up the other three legs of this desk chair. *Grrrrrrrrrrrrrrrr!* Two down and two to go. I can only hope there is enough chair for me to get through this chapter. No worries—there's plenty of other stuff around here for me to take my frustrations out on. *I am dog; hear me roar!*

As you may have guessed, the human remains out-of-town. *Who has "business" that lasts two days? Too much fiber in her diet or not enough?* Anyway, I decided to rifle through the human's notes after breakfast this morning. It turns out that this chapter was to be all about Buffy (entirely predictably so). I'm guessing there will be one on Carla Mae, too. I question my judgment in letting the human "help" with this project at all. She really is on her very own little planet sometimes. Nonetheless, I do get where the human is coming from. I think I should warn you though—I *bawled* when I read the human's chicken scratch. I thought I misunderstood or misread something. I went to Buffy. She confirmed the worst. I bawled more and then I got angry. *Then* the proverbial light bulb lit up and suddenly I became aware of the human's crazy infatuation with dogs (her own as well as every stray that has ever crossed her path). My human is a hero. She doesn't have it within herself to walk away from a situation where she knows she can do some good.

That's the terrible thing about heroes and knowledge—once they have the knowledge, they can't go back in time and suddenly *not* have it. The heroes become aware and it becomes their responsibility to do whatever is in their power to help. Knowledge sucks that way for heroes.

There are few things sadder in this life than a persecuted puppy. *Down with clowns! May the fleas of one thousand bull dogs infest your armpits as you grow weary of your 10x10 cell with cold floors and no treats in sight!* Okay, that was a little harsh—even for me. Admittedly, I do have some anger issues to work through. Buffy is my sister and forgiveness for these lousy excuses for a life form isn't coming easily. I overheard someone once say, "Not forgiving another is the equivalent of *you* taking poison and hoping *they'll* die." I have no idea what that means. I'm guessing it's going in the direction of forgiveness being divine maybe. Yeah, I dunno. What I do know is that if Buffy can forgive and move on, so can I. Perhaps it's easier to forgive than forget.

I feel closer to Buffy than ever before, even though I have always considered her to be my second in charge, my silent (and sometimes *not* so silent) partner, not to mention the lady of the house. She sets a standard of grace and etiquette, which I respect. Then she'll fart. *What's up with that? It's just gross.*

Anyway, when I first met Buffy, all I saw was this entirely lovely Cocker Spaniel with a shiny, flowing coat and pink bows placed daintily above her ears. She was grateful to have a strong male presence in the house and seemed to appreciate my energy. I'd run around and around the table, showing her how I could pick up speed with each lap, momentum fueling my every stride. Buffy still enjoys watching me and encouraging me with her kind and gentle nods of approval, never really wanting to join in and being completely content to observe and applaud.

Up until this morning, I was completely ignorant of Buffy's past. And right up to and including this moment, I wish I could go back in time and *not* know that Buffy was severely abused by two men who are currently doing time in prison for their heinous acts. No punishment will ever be great enough. *I know, I know—"think forgiveness, MaGoo." I resolve to replace my anger with greater security measures! That'll do it.*

I now understand why Buffy has always been so timid and especially fearful of men. It's not an impossible situation, it just takes her a little while to establish trust and warm up to someone new. But by golly when she does, Buffy latches on and loves with all her might. I also now understand her love of bows and ribbons and trips to the groomer. She feels loved and cared for and pampered. I think it makes her feel beautiful and helps her forget where she came from.

So many of Buffy's early puppyhood years remain painful memories, but it's those memories that inspire her to enjoy the moment, live for the day, and treasure even the smallest of joys. Buffy isn't into playing ball; she'd rather dig through our basket of toys and collect all of *her* bones, gently stacking them upon her favorite pillow—trophies,

reminding her of her unique place in this universe. No matter what this life may bring, my favorite image of Buffy will remain of her chasing birds in the park—her shiny coat flowing, her body almost gliding across the field of green grass as hundreds of birds scramble to take flight. Buffy's spirit seems to take flight as well. At those moments, she has nothing but joy in her heart. She loves and is loved and nothing else matters. Buffy finds the strength to forgive and to forget, and to always remember the lady God intended her to be. She's freaking classy that way.

I know the human has our best interest in mind, but does anyone else think the vet isn't the best idea out there? Dang—it does seem like bad stuff can happen there. I've not had any unfortunate luck in that area personally, but my sisters look as if they may all share that same curious vet allergy—vet-itis? Buffy was at one medical facility for four very long nights. The human took us to visit her. I wondered why we couldn't bring Buffy home with us, and then I saw she was connected to a machine that appeared to be allowing some kind of fluid to drip through a tube and into her body. I am *not* making this up. It was weird, and Buffy, while tolerant, did *not* enjoy it. She belonged home with us, where I could keep a close watch on her. I find myself panicked and pacing when one of my sisters is out of sight. I have no earthly idea how the human expects me to provide

24/7 protection, when she can't keep all of us under one roof. Dude—she's not even here right now.

Moving right along… the human purchased a big, fluffy, over-stuffed bed and a toy dog for Buffy when she came home from the hospital. I *love* that bed! And that stuffed dog *rocks*! It's still my favorite toy today. My sisters all want me to curl up with them in their beds, so I get to try everyone's stuff out. Carla Mae is so finicky often when I curl up next to her, she'll get up and go to another bed (mine is usually available). Naturally, the girls all feel safer with me around. I *am* fearless and strong. I maintain order and take no crap from anyone. I *eat* clowns for breakfast. *Grrrrrrrrrrr! Woof!*

I watch over Buffy constantly and follow her around. When I get tired of doing that, I bark and bark until she follows me. For the most part, she does a decent job keeping up. But every now and again, she'll poof up,

get all agitated, and walk away grumbling. I know this to be a good time to leave her alone. A guy needs to respect those boundaries if he doesn't want his tail chewed out.

Buffy makes the funniest noises when she's sleeping. I just know she is dreaming about something *good* and I have to know what it is. So I wake her up. Seems she would be more understanding. But as time goes on, I feel like it takes more and more to wake her and get her moving. Some mornings I break into a round of "Good Morning Merry Sunshine" for her and she'll just lay there and yawn. *Rise and shine! Greet the day with your smile! It's time to eat and run and play! Gooooood morning, Merry Sunshine. How did you wake so soon? You scared the little stars away and shined away the moon!* How can anyone *not* love being serenaded at the very crack of dawn? This is an awesome, luxury service I'm providing. She's probably just trying to lay still because she's secretly recording my vocal extravaganza with plans to sell it on eBay. That *must* be it. Quality *is* important. It's the only logical reason someone would feign boredom over my exuberant performance. Just trying to keep the white noise down to a minimum. Still, I always stand very close and sing loudly because I do know her hearing and eyesight aren't what they used to be. That's me. I'm a giver.

Getting back to the whole hero deal going on with the human (I think she gets that from me): one day, Buffy, Betty Boop, the human, and I were all on our way to the groomers (this was before Carla Mae's time) with pretty pink things for the girls to adorn themselves with afterwards and a sporty blue sweater and scarf for me. *I look soooooooooo sharp in that scarf! No frills MaGoo, coming through, coming through. Make some room for the stylish Mr. MaGoo.* So we're totally pumped up and excited and then out of nowhere, right in the curve of the freaking road, is this wonderful yellow Labrador. The human stops our vehicle and another spectacular yellow Lab appears. It was *crazy!* The human gets out of the car and is on her phone. I'm barking and alerting passersby of the potentially hazardous situation. Buffy is freaking out and fretting uncontrollably. Betty Boop is sleeping. And the human's making calls all over town, while trying to hold onto the labs. It was a hugger-mugger of a goat-roping if I ever saw one. It was intense. I totally puked on the way to the groomers afterwards. Eventually the two yellow labs made it home to the humans who had raised them since puppyhood. I had given my all and it was just another happy ending in The MaGoo Chronicles.

I'll, of course, continue to maintain a secure 360 degree perimeter around my sisters and the human whenever we're out and about for a walk. Occasionally the human gets caught up in the leashes, becomes confused and instead of holding the girls close and letting me run to do my job to fend off an opposing German Shepherd, she holds us *all* back. Clueless. The woman is just *clueless* sometimes. How in the world am I supposed to be able to do my job when I'm being restrained? Clueless, I tell ya.

We have a lot of fun and a lot of great memories together, although with Buffy's emotional and physical issues, Betty Boop's water on the brain, me with my rare, occasional, and hugely *minor* ear problems—at times it's more than the human can handle. And dang—we haven't even gotten to Carla Mae yet!

Yep. Carla Mae is a trip. *Wait a second! Did you hear that? It's her car! I swear it's her car—I know that sound. She's home! She's home! She's home! Woof!* Well kids, I've got some human-jumping and greeting that needs tended to. I'll catch y'all on the flip side.

Chapter Six

A Raspy House Guest

Carla Mae, Carla Mae. What can I say about the bold and daring Carla Mae? You guys are going to find this hard to believe, but Carla Mae and I didn't get along so great in the beginning. *Woof!* That girl wore me out. I saw her as a fellow *Lhasa Apso—a peer, and perhaps my expectations of immediate friendship were a bit out of whack. For you humans, it would be like when you meet another redhead or someone who shares your name and you say, "Dang, my name's Karen too. You must be cool." It's an unrealistic expectation, because all Karens are not cool and all Lhasa Apsos are not me. Sad, but true.*

Before I go any further, I suppose I should let you guys know the human is home. What a nutcase. She's in freaky-geeky mode—running around like a chicken with its head cut off. (Whoa – I'm just realizing what a horrible expression that is! But if y'all have made it this far, I'm

guessing you're tough enough to handle it.) The human is making calls,
and giving medications, falling short on the doggy treats and completely
overlooking the fact that we're writing a book! Holy cow, if I waited for
her, this thing would never be finished. She asked what I was doing on the
computer earlier and I barked out: "Surfing the net." Can we say
"gullible"? Try surfing the net, watching some YouTube videos, doing
some online shopping (gotta love the Amazon one-click thing!) and kicking
out three chapters in the meantime. But the little flibbertigibbet of a
human prefers to spend her time nervously pacing about like a long-tailed
cat in a room full of rocking chairs.

Back to my feisty little sister, Carla Mae. As I have previously
mentioned, we're all pretty used to an ongoing flow of foster dogs through
our home. We lay low and allow the other dogs some space and time to
relax. We're hugely tolerant because it's all so temporary. Before one has
time to worry or fret or remotely consider the future with one of these
transient canines, they're gone—hopefully to somewhere wonderful and
happily perfect for them. There's rarely any serious conflict or threat. I
show the strays around, help them adjust to my precision-perfect schedule,
answer questions, and before you know it, they're off on their own brand

new adventure equipped with whatever knowledge I have had the opportunity to impart on them.

Not so with Carla Mae. Not even a little bit. She was such an angry and aggressive little cuss. When she saw sweet, innocent Betty Boop in all her defenselessness, Carla Mae sought out to attack and destroy the weaker animal. *What is up with that?! Not in my home, buddy! Arf!* Carla Mae lunged toward Betty Boop with snake-like accuracy—growling and snarling and baring her teeth. *Both* Buffy and I ran to the rescue. Not only no, but *heck no!* We let Carla Mae know that we do *not* tolerate that kind of behavior around here. We are not bullies and we do not hurt each other. And from a compeer Lhasa Apso—well, you can imagine my disappointment.

It was an uphill battle and required additional security measures on my part. Buffy and I took shifts keeping an especially close watch on Betty Boop, with me taking the lion's share of responsibility (though I must admit that Buffy turned out to be quite the warrior when someone she loved was threatened). I barely slept and found myself easily startled by the slightest of noises. I kept a vigilant watch over Betty Boop and was all over Carla Mae like a cheap suit if she so much as looked at my little sister for too long. I hate to admit it, but I was ready for our guest to move on and couldn't contain my excitement when the fateful call came, followed by the human's tears, and a bittersweet good-bye.

YEA! But before I could grasp what was happening, the human was *welcoming* Carla Mae into *our* family. *Whoa!! What did I miss? Phone call—check. Tears—check. Where's the "good-bye"?!* Something had come unhinged. And in that very instant, my world changed forever.

The human had adopted Carla Mae. I was devastated. We already had three dogs and a human in the house and Carla Mae didn't seem to respect or appreciate any of us. The incident was completely unprecedented and for the first time in my life, I was unprepared. I had no words, no action, no thought—no game plan whatsoever. I sunk into a deep despair knowing my days (and nap times) would forever be filled by the never-ending need to keep Carla Mae from harming Betty Boop. As the human shed her tears, I continued to sink deeper and deeper…

Weeks passed and my spirit ached for fun—simple, non-confrontational fun. Buffy no longer tolerated my antics as she once had and Betty Boop slept often (though even when awake, the little angel was no match for my brand of rough-n-tumble play). It sucked that the one dog who might remotely prove to be a decent playmate was the one dog I just couldn't like (despite the fact that *the human* had apparently grown quite fond of Carla Mae).

One day, I couldn't take it any longer so I walked over to Carla Mae and playfully chewed on her ear. To my surprise she smiled and nudged me back. Then I chewed some more. Before I knew it, we were up on our hind legs playing patty-cake. In all my excitement, I suddenly lost my balance and fell backwards onto the floor. Carla Mae froze—fear etched across her snout as if she had done something wrong. I howled! Then we both laughed and simultaneously realized what a waste of time being angry and bitter really is.

In time Carla Mae became a good playmate and worthy boxing opponent. Looking back, with her spunk, natural balance and sense of rhythm (not to mention having such a talented instructor as myself), I should've guessed she'd turn out to be a fine dancer as well. Carla Mae knows how to put some wiggle in her walk and rock like a pop star. It never occurred to me who Carla Mae was before she came here. I only thought of who she was at the moment and the mystery of who she might become in time.

Occasionally I'd eavesdrop on the human's phone conversations in regard to Carla Mae. Prior to coming to live with us, Carla Mae stayed in a very loud and abusive home (which explained why she was so easily rattled). Carla Mae was the red-headed step child of the Dysfunction Family—on the corner of Rock Road and Hard Place Lane. Household frustrations were taken out on her and she learned early in life what a powerful defense mechanism biting can be.

The human struggled at times with Carla Mae as much as Buffy and I did. Just when you'd think all was well, Carla Mae would revert back to her mistrustful ways. The human eventually called in a professional canine communicator.

Interesting that you humans need a professional's help to communicate with your dogs and we dogs have managed on our own for centuries. Do you see us hiring someone to tell us what you're saying? Are

we cleaning up after you and preparing meals? Paying the mortgage? You

put roofs over heads and provide food and beverage at no monetary cost

to us. You walk us and clean up after us. Really—who is the superior

species here?

Anyway, it took a professional to relay to the human that it

aggravates me when my authority is challenged. (It's not like it would take

a brain scientist or a rocket surgeon to figure that one out.) She further

said that Carla Mae struggled with boundaries and was unsure of her place

on the family totem pole. The canine communicator was brilliant in her

analysis and all she had to do was listen. I remain amazed that most

humans don't speak a lick of dog and yet you expect us to understand *your*

every word. Many thanks to the millions of dog communicators out there

who devote their time to better the human race via canine conversation. It

really is about time.

Thank goodness Carla Mae has me as a primary influence. I taught

her how to use her energy to dance and to play. And she learned to let go

of her anger and forgive those in her past. And yes, Carla Mae learned to

stop biting too… I mean, unless she's really, really provoked.

One lazy Saturday afternoon, the human took me and Buffy and Carla Mae out for a walk around the lake. The sun felt warm on our backs and the grass felt cool beneath my paws. You couldn't ask for a more blissful day—at least until this German Shepherd named King came along. *"King" my furry butt!* King lunged at us and strained hard against his human's grasp on the leash. I heard the old, familiar sound of Carla Mae's growl. I *knew* the two of us could take him. Buffy would be tucked safely behind the human, as is her way in threatening situations. I pushed to break free to put that stupid dog "King" in his place, but as I looked over my shoulder I noticed that Carla Mae was not lunging forward, but rather backing up as she growled. Her growl was menacing, her teeth—threatening, her bark—fear-inducing. But it was her eyes that betrayed her, as she backed away from King Dumb-head. They glazed over fearfully—a single tear formed and hurried away to find refuge in Carla Mae's fur. She shook it off and continued to bark fiercely—hoping no one noticed.

It was at that very moment I realized Carla Mae was not just an angry, aggressive little cuss I taught to play and dance and cut loose. I saw Carla Mae for the first time as she really was—a scared puppy who learned to mistrust those around her and who learned self-preservation the only way she knew how—by biting first and asking questions later. She was a frightened little dog who eventually found a greater lesson in letting go and learning to laugh and play and yes, of course—dance. Carla Mae found unconditional love in our family and along the way, she learned to trust. Anyway, as for Dim-Bulb King, cooler heads prevailed that day and, lucky for him, his human finally dragged him away from us. But I sure learned something about my new sister that day.

This learning to trust thing—it was good for Carla Mae because once in a blue moon the human drops the ball completely and we all must trust in each other. One time (due to a schedule miscommunication), my sisters and I were home alone for thirty hours. It rocked. We watched what we wanted on TV without interruption. We kept fluids to a minimum and managed to hold our water till the human got home—which was quite the sight to see. Whoa, she was out of control! Crazy hair flying, flailing arms, shrieks and intermittent tears, bouts of laughter, unnecessary apologies. Dude—we were perfectly fine. Really. It was funny to see the human freak out.

As for Carla Mae and Buffy—I think they made their peace. Carla Mae learned to respect our home and our family and to love little Betty Boop as much as the rest of us do. Beautiful Buffy (the lady of the house) ended up welcoming Cutie Cutie Carla Mae as our princess, warrior, and playmate.

As for me—Carla Mae turned out to be a competitive little tomboy and fair adversary. We love to play Kibble Attack—a game that involves her patiently planning preemptive Kibble invasions, only to be taken off guard by a MaGoo surprise maneuver, overrun and forever a close *second* only to me. She's quite the copycat as well, often mimicking our moves. I'm not sure if she's mocking us all, doing the "when in Rome thing", or a little of both. What I do know is that I have learned to love Carla Mae and Carla Mae has learned to accept love and even try to nudge in on my petting time with the human and even with random human strangers in the house. She is loved and cared for and Carla Mae is no longer afraid… well, maybe a *little* afraid of King Crazy Dog, but who wouldn't be? Other than me, of course.

Cutie Cutie Carla Mae—curled up and resting in her favorite spot. Think I'll go chew on her ear for awhile.

Chapter Seven

Betty Boop: A Blessing in Disguise

Oh my goodness, Mr. MaGoo! What have you done now? Wow. I had no idea you could get so much writing done while at the same time managing to so completely chew up my office chair...

Reading through Mr. MaGoo's literary contributions while I was away brought back so many memories. Even though I had a feeling that the journey I started ten years ago might be a challenging one, I really had no idea where it would take me—where it takes me still. I also had no idea at the time that even though my adoption of Betty Boop was a blessing for her, it would ultimately be so much more of a blessing for me.

When I drove to Anaheim to pick up Betty Boop, I knew she was a special-needs dog. I also knew that I could help. I was determined to improve the quality of her health and her life with good nutrition and positive thinking. But I was unaware of her blindness, unaware of the seizures to come, unaware of the water on her brain, the necessary medicines, and ultimately the amount of care this tiny puppy would require. I was also unaware of the qualities I would soon discover in myself, qualities that Betty Boop would help reveal.

In no time I discovered Betty Boop enjoyed being held and would spend a few minutes squirming in my arms before settling on a comfortable position and drifting off to sleep. When she was truly happy, she'd cock her head and stick her tongue out slightly—staring through blind eyes. I've questioned my decisions a million times and have often been overwhelmed by the demands of caring for her, but when Betty Boop, all of just over three pounds, tilts her head and gives me that expression of contentment, my doubts vanish.

Soon after I adopted Betty Boop, Dr. Hilinski suggested a visit to the same neurologist I had taken Gizmo to, believing the neurologist could run tests that might rule out certain neurological issues and give us some additional insight. "Sure," I said to Dr. Hilinski, "that sounds like a great plan." I was unrealistically optimistic. Perhaps the cure would be a simple procedure, or nutritional supplement, or maybe a single-dose medicine! I had a bounce in my step as I walked into the neurologist's office—my hopes set high on some miraculous elixir.

The doctor greeted me and inquired about Gizmo, who had, by then, exceeded the doctor's two-week prognosis with no real signs of slowing down anytime soon. The doctor seemed surprised that Gizmo was still with us at all, referencing the size of her tumor. "So much for *your* prediction," I thought to myself. Still, I felt comforted by our familiar conversation and chalked up Gizmo's beating the odds to a positive mental attitude.

"Well, what do we have here, Kelly?" The doctor motioned towards Betty Boop.

"This is Betty Boop," I replied, "and Betty Boop seems to be able to walk only in tight circles." The neurologist held Betty Boop and gently rubbed her forehead as I talked. "Dr. Hilinski referred me to you so we could do some tests and figure out what's going on with her. I can't seem to get her to walk in a straight line no matter what I try."

The doctor continued to palpate Betty Boop's head as he spoke in even tones. "That's because she was born with a soft spot, right here. It's likely she has water on the brain."

"What do you mean, doctor?" I was completely unfamiliar with the condition and its severity. The doctor took my thumb and had me feel the slightly indented, soft area of Betty Boop's skull. Evidently, her brain never fully and properly developed.

"What can we do?" I asked. I was ready for answers and ready for action. What I wasn't ready for was the doctor's response.

"Based on the severity of her condition and what you're telling me, we really can't do much," he said rather matter-of-factly. I stared at him blankly as he continued. "Your best option at this point is to put her to sleep."

"Wha—? Why?"

"I'm afraid Betty Boop will never be a normal dog."

"Well…what do you mean by 'normal'?" I questioned. The doctor paused and I could tell he was looking for a way to help me better understand Betty Boop's condition.

"Just think of her as a Down's Syndrome child," he said at last. "She has severe retardation. Severe. You'll never be able to play ball with her or take her for a walk. And at best, she might live to be six months old. Put her to sleep, Kelly. It's really the best thing." I stared at him, confused and hurt. How, I wondered vaguely, could someone think of giving up on a living, breathing dog so quickly? But the doctor continued: "Afterwards, Kelly, it would be greatly appreciated if you would consent to donating her brain to the clinic. We'd like to examine it, perhaps learn more about this disease."

Of course my brother Shawn had been a Down's syndrome child and so I knew a thing or two about the condition. And one thing I knew is that we don't throw people away who are so afflicted, and I wouldn't entertain any thoughts that my Betty Boop should be treated any differently.

"We don't put our children who are born with Down's Syndrome or other mental or physical ailments to sleep," I said, trying to maintain my composure. But I suddenly couldn't stop thinking of Shawn's smiling face, and it wasn't easy. "We give them a chance." I picked Betty Boop up and stormed out of the neurologist's office. Betty Boop had been a part of my life for such a short period of time—only days, really. But I was already hopelessly attached. I drove home in tears. I hadn't expected the diagnosis nor the analogy that came with it. I called my sister Colleen who was equally as shocked by the doctor's words.

"What are you going to do, Kelly?" Colleen sounded as bewildered as I felt.

"I have no earthly idea, Colleen. I guess I really just need a little time to digest all of this."

I spent the entire weekend doing just that. I second-guessed my decision to keep her alive. I cried. I did my best to think logically and unselfishly. *How much time do we really have? Will I honestly be up to the challenge? Am I doing what's fair to her? Am I even being fair to myself?* Caring for Gizmo was still taking a lot of my time and energy. *Does this make sense? Am I doing the right thing?* Buffy was still new to the house and needed me as well. *Am I even capable of caring for all these dogs?* Through all my questions and doubts about the only thing I was sure of was that I didn't want to donate Betty Boop's brain to science. It just seemed too cold and clinical to imagine this little innocent puppy being dissected like a lab rat immediately after being euthanized.

As the weekend progressed, I found myself leaning more and more towards the idea that the neurologist was right. I was beginning to feel over my head. Maybe putting Betty Boop to sleep was what I needed to do and what was best for all concerned. By Monday morning I decided that Betty Boop was in no condition to live a quality life. I made an appointment with Dr. Hilinski to put her to sleep.

I gathered up all of Betty Boop's toys and bedding materials and any other evidence of her two weeks' time with me. I didn't want the reminders. I showed up on time for our final appointment with the doctor— trying to be strong, trying not to cry. I knew I had to let Betty Boop go. But as I carried her in, she looked up at me with that contented expression of hers and I felt my heart breaking.

Dr. Hilinski entered the examination room and began reviewing Betty Boop's chart, occasionally asking me a question—which I managed to answer in one or two word sentences. "Yup." "Uh-huh." "Nope." "Correct." It was taking everything I had to hold back the flood of emotions I was experiencing. I just wanted it to be over.

"Well Kelly, we do have some options." I couldn't hold back the tears, as much as I tried. I was ready to let go. I'd struggled and had come to a tough conclusion. The thought that there were options I had not considered threw me back on the emotional rollercoaster I had been riding all weekend. "You're not ready to do this, are you Kelly?" Dr. Hilinski quietly asked as he peered over the rim of his glasses, his compassionate eyes meeting mine. I shook my head and sobbed uncontrollably.

Dr. Hilinski pushed back his dark hair, returning his glance to the chart before him, and we began to weigh our options. A shunt was considered, to drain the water off of Betty Boop's brain, but due to the advanced state of her condition, the shunt may not have worked and could even have ended up creating additional complications, thus disqualifying her for the procedure altogether. And so the doctor gently told me that—*perhaps*—with a lot of work and dedication, Betty Boop might be able to live a life, albeit a short one, with at least some measure of quality to it. "It won't be easy Kelly. It's going to take a lot of patience."

"I don't care! I'll do whatever it takes," I replied, not remotely knowing what the promise I was making would actually entail.

Dr. Hilinski was convinced Betty Boop wouldn't make it to her first birthday, but with extraordinary care, she might have at least some time, perhaps a few months, maybe more. He reiterated what the neurologist had said—Betty Boop would never be a dog who could chase a ball or go for a walk—but said that she might be able to have a quality of life "suitable for her". Of course there were no guarantees. But I didn't need guarantees. I believed that love and patience could conquer whatever problems would be thrown our way. I would be loyal, consistent with her medicines and committed to keeping her as healthy and happy as was possible. Even if I really didn't know at the time what all of that meant.

Dr. Hilinski warned me that seizures were probable. I was still teary-eyed and grateful as I held my little Betty Boop in his office that day—I'd been prepared to put her to sleep and now there was renewed hope. I didn't spend so much as two seconds wondering what a seizure would be like. I took her back home that day. I nurtured her, and tried to help her eat on her own. I had no idea what I was doing. I only knew that I had to try.

Taking care of Betty Boop would turn out to be a grueling, time-consuming process. I canceled trips home, family get-togethers, and time with friends. On one occasion I'd missed a morning flight back home to see my family in Pennsylvania for a planned vacation. Just as I was leaving, Betty Boop had a severe seizure. I called home and told my dad I wasn't going to be able to make my flight but that I would try to catch another one later that night. He understood. I sat with Betty Boop most of the day and when the sitter finally arrived and I began feeling like my little ones were in capable hands, I caught the red-eye home that night. But this wasn't Betty Boop's first seizure and over time I've gotten more capable of managing them— medically, intellectually, emotionally.

It wasn't a month after bringing Betty Boop home that she had her very first seizure. It was about 9:00 P.M. and I was finishing up some laundry. Betty Boop was on the floor circling around, seemingly happy in her own little world. Then out of nowhere she cried out—almost a scream really. I looked to see her suddenly flailing on the floor. My immediate reaction was to pick her up. She was slobbering uncontrollably, her eyes were fixated, and her temperature was noticeably elevated. She lost control of her bodily functions. I was confused and scared. I had no earthly idea what to do, save for just holding her. And then as quickly as it started, it stopped and she lay limp in my arms. It was, perhaps, the longest ninety seconds of my life.

Betty Boop and I were back at Rolling Hills Pet Hospital seeking the advice of Dr. Keith Hilinski the very next morning. I learned that what I had witnessed was, in fact, a seizure and we'd need to put her on appropriate medicines.

I'm not certain if Betty Boop simply outgrew the bladder and bowel accidents while I hold her during a seizure, or if perhaps the medicines have helped to alleviate that issue, but that's one problem we at least no longer have. She still has seizures, maybe one every three to five weeks. I began a journal to document them and to help the doctor prescribe medication accordingly. The seizures generally last thirty to ninety seconds. After an especially bad one she'll lose her appetite and it'll take two days to a week before she's back up to speed. The seizures are often emotionally painful to watch. I pick her up. I dose her with Phenobarbital and give her plenty of water to rehydrate her. Then I hold her until she falls asleep. When I'm not there for a seizure, she paces in circles and often ends up with a respiratory infection from aspirating saliva and backwash.

Betty Boop was put on a lifetime of medications—Furosemide to reduce swelling around her brain, Phenobarbital and Potassium Bromine to control the potential seizures. There was much trial and error with medicines for the first six months, maybe even a year. Eventually the right cocktail was created.

At first, I devoted a great deal of my time caring for Betty Boop, fortunately being able to work primarily from home. Before long, all of my life revolved around her medicines and daily dosing routines. I quickly discovered the value of waterproof sheets and padding and spent a lot of time doing laundry. Betty Boop would never be house-broken and I resolved to always give her a clean place to sleep. After Mr. MaGoo joined the clan, I purchased a playpen for Betty Boop to make sure she wasn't trampled. It also helped me to contain her messiness to one area.

Betty Boop and I spent a lot of time at Dr. Hilinski's office that first year, so much time that upon the milestone of Betty Boop's first birthday—a day she was predicted to never reach—the doctor's staff joked with me about naming a suite after us. Thousands of dollars and hundreds of hours were spent caring for the treasured angel—so small and frail and loving.

In addition to the seizures, Betty Boop has produced her share of other frightening moments. During a routine visit to Dr. Hilinski's, with Betty Boop in the examination room, I overheard the office manager announce to others in the waiting area: "We'll be with you shortly. We have an emergency in the back."

"Erica?" I said to the receptionist, "what's going on?" Erica didn't look at me, instead mumbling that she'd be right with me and then heading straight for the back room. For the next twenty minutes I paced. I knew the emergency had something to do with my Betty Boop. Eventually, when the staff resurfaced, I was told, "Betty Boop flat-lined. We were able to revive her heart, but she's not breathing on her own."

"I want to go back with her!" I was ushered to the back where I saw my little Betty Boop lying motionless. She'd apparently had some internal hemorrhaging which caused her heart to stop beating. The bleeding was controlled and her heart was now beating again but her little lungs just wouldn't seem to kick in. I called my manager to let him know I wouldn't be available for the remainder of the day.

Then I called the guy I had been dating for the previous three months, hoping, I guess, for some compassion and a little understanding. I'd been there for him, after all. It's what people in relationships do for each other, or so I thought. Apparently I was hoping for too much. After my tearful description of events he asked simply if I planned to always be with a dog "that poops all over herself" and if instead it might be better to "call it quits." After all, he said, "your vet bill must be soaring. You've gotta be spending $1500 a month on that dog. It's ridiculous, Kelly."

I choked back my tears and disappointment and told him I'd call him again when I was home. Mr. MaGoo, you might have noticed, is fond of using the word "clowns" to describe certain human beings. I think this guy qualifies.

Meanwhile, in the back of the veterinary office, Dr. Hilinski was using a coffee stirrer for Betty Boop's oxygen supply as they couldn't keep a good enough seal on a mask to allow the necessary oxygen in. My little angel was turning blue. Dr. Hilinski turned to me and said gravely, "In thirty minutes, we'll have to call it, Kelly. I'm sorry." I wanted to cry but knew I had to be strong. I knew Betty Boop would be able to feel my energy.

When it was Gizmo's time, I told her it was okay to go. Maybe the opposite approach would work this time. With two minutes left in the doctor's grace period, I leaned in close to Betty Boop. "Mommy's here," I whispered. "It's not your time to go yet. Not yet...not yet, my Betty Boop." Suddenly she inhaled deeply, and then began breathing on her own. It was a miracle. "Amazing," Dr. Hilinski said, and then repeated, "*amazing.*"

It was decided that the best thing for Betty Boop would be to come home that night with an IV in place. We both desperately needed a bath and I ached for the comfort of home. Carla Mae, Mr. MaGoo, and Buffy all greeted us at the door to make sure Betty Boop was okay. I cleaned Betty Boop up and got her comfortable before drawing a hot bath for myself. My day had been long and I wanted to wash away some of the tension before calling "the clown" to let him know we were back home.

My soon to be ex-boyfriend offered to bring dinner over. Exhausted and hungry, I accepted but I soon came to understand that he would never be the guy I could count on for emotional support. Needless to say our relationship ended shortly thereafter. This was just the first of a string of relationships to end as a direct or indirect result of a potential boyfriend's reaction to Betty Boop. I don't think one would ever consider saying to the parent of a Down's Syndrome child, "Wow, how tragic", but time and again that's what I hear with respect to Betty Boop. Someday maybe I'll hear, "Wow, she's a little miracle, isn't she? How inspiring!" Maybe that'll be the right guy.

I held Betty Boop all night as she slept soundlessly in my arms after that traumatic day. The next morning found us curled up together with her perfectly fine, as if nothing at all had happened. The next three days were filled with all-day vet visits and IV fluids and more pacing. She seemed completely stable on her last day at Dr. Hilinski's office and the staff surprised me when they brought her up to me in a brand new "Diva-doo." She looked stunning.

For months to follow, whether having her teeth cleaned or blood drawn, I would not leave Betty Boop alone at the vets. I had become her preferred veterinary assistant and often she would not allow anyone else to hold her while in with the doctor.

Over time I learned by trial and error how best to feed Betty Boop. I sit with her twice a day for thirty to forty-five minutes to help her eat. Her sense of smell is very keen and she knows food when she gets a whiff of it. I float her Kibble in a small bowl of water and have her straddle a blanket with her head elevated and with the bowl in front of her, her head and bowl at the same level—a technique I came up with one day when I had inadvertently left her food beside some phone books to answer the phone. When I turned back to look at her she was on the phone books, eating on her own. I don't even remember who I was talking to but I hung

up without thinking, grabbed my camera, and captured the moment.

While she eats I watch and encourage her. As she laps up the

water and pounds the Kibble down with her tongue, I fluff the remaining

Kibble up for her. It occurs to me that I may never have learned to sit still

otherwise. In being forced to learn patience, I have learned to relax more. I

have Betty Boop to thank for this.

In 2007 we had a brain scan done to get a better picture of Betty

Boop's true condition. The staff besieged me afterwards in the waiting

room with questions: What are you feeding her? How are you able to take

care of her? *How is it this dog is even alive?* Seeing my bewildered

expression, somebody finally let me know what the scan revealed: Betty

Boop has less than one-percent functional brain matter. It seemed

impossible. By everything known to science Betty Boop should not have survived past a year. Whatever it is you're doing, the staff said, keep doing it.

In my opinion, it's no great secret. Betty Boop simply has the will to live. She responds well to me and she eats and drinks on her own. She perks up when I come home from travel and always seems comforted by my presence and my touch.

Since business travel is sometimes unavoidable, I have come to rely on an amazing dog sitter. Caring for dogs is her passion, and she has many clients to show for it. When I'm on the road, she'll visit three times a day to make sure Betty Boop takes her medications, in addition to being there to care for all the other members of the family.

Making sure Betty Boop gets her necessary medications continues to be paramount. Her very life depends on it. Everyone gets fed around Betty Boop's schedule with Betty Boop getting fed last. While her Kibble floats and becomes soft enough for her, I change her bedding and begin laundry. While she eats, I sit on the steps to keep an eye on her while I give the other dogs some attention.

Betty Boop, as you might imagine, can be quite the messy eater and when she's done, Mr. MaGoo and Carla Mae race for the leftovers. Nine times out of ten, Mr. MaGoo gets there first.

Betty Boop has moments of stunning progress. This past Christmas she broke out walking in a straight line—like a normal dog. It was our Christmas miracle. She wasn't able to maintain it for long, but it showed me what can happen with a little nurturing, a little encouragement, and a lot of love.

Respiratory infections continue to be an issue for her. We use a vaporizer, Vick's, and "Little Noses" to help keep her sinuses and lungs clear. She loves lying out in the sun and being showered with love and attention. Her bathwater needs to be lukewarm—not hot, not cold. She's picky and knows what she likes and what she dislikes. If she doesn't like the way you're holding her, for instance, she can be quite the little wiggle worm until you get it just right. She rarely barks yet she communicates easily and in some ways I think she might just be the toughest one in the pack.

The time spent caring for Betty Boop and the others has not been without its share of difficulties with regard to how I am able to interact with the outside world. Even though friends and family members have said they understand, they still often seem put off when I can't stay longer at a party or take a weekend to travel. Due to health issues, I've been unable to have children of my own. Frequently people seem to want to judge the choices I've made when they discover I have four high maintenance dogs. One evening recently while having dinner at a friend's house, her husband commented, "You have so much love to give, Kelly. It seems like such a pity and a waste you don't have children. Don't get me wrong—I love dogs, too. But why not share some of this love with a child? Why not adopt?" Understanding my choices would be nice, but I think all any of us really wants is to be loved and accepted as we are. Not that my choices need justification, but I find my life, with work and travel and four dogs, to be challenging and fulfilling enough at this time. I tried to explain this as best I could, even though I really wanted to tell him to piss off for the presumptuousness of his question.

"I'm not saying 'never' to adoption. Just not right now. Not while I feel like I'm already spreading myself thin," I managed to answer. I haven't exactly been in a hurry to accept another dinner invitation from my friend and her husband.

I've become a firm believer that one must return the unconditional love that their pets have always given them. Caring for these guys brings me more joy than I could ever have imagined. I'm the center of their universe and they of mine. I feel purpose and direction and love. I have learned to sit still and have faith. I have witnessed miracles. I have sacrificed some, and I have gained much. Betty Boop taught me patience and devotion and the rewards of doing whatever is needed for those whom you love.

Every now and again I sneak away for a facial or to have my nails done, but I'm always anxious to hurry home to my furry family. No one knows what the future holds and I don't have any way of knowing when that last dog kiss or puppy snuggle might be. For now, my time is about them. Betty Boop has been nothing less than an adorable angel and a miracle in my life. It's by choice that I remain here for her, and my interest in whether the rest of the world completely understands seems to fade with each passing, love-filled day.

Chapter Eight

Beautiful Buffy

Oh, Mr. MaGoo. You are such a drama queen! "The fleas of one thousand bull dogs"? Really? (What I find most troubling are all the paw prints on my monitor and what appears to be dog drool on my mouse...)

At any rate, as much as I appreciate Mr. MaGoo's descriptions, allow me to tell you a little more about our Buffy. First off, the one word that's consistently used to describe her by all those who meet her is *beautiful*—and that she is. Buffy is a lovely Cocker Spaniel. She is kind and matronly to the other dogs, with a most elegant manner. If one didn't know better, they'd think Mr. MaGoo's story of the two horrible men who had done mean and nasty things to Buffy was fiction. I only wish it was.

To be plain, Buffy was sexually abused. It's funny when you think about how people who are sick and twisted are often referred to as "animals." I have a house full of animals. I've been around animals my whole life. I think I know what an animal is, and it's an insult to animals to somehow equate perverts like those who abused Buffy with anything whatsoever in the animal kingdom. From the most regal lion to the lowliest maggot, these freaks don't belong. There's a category all its own for the likes of them.

The monsters that had Buffy made certain there would be no escape for her, allowing the fur of her front paws to grow together so that she was unable to run, barely even able to walk. It's difficult to even conceive of that kind of mentality. I shudder to think how long the abuse might have continued had a neighbor in their apartment complex not heard Buffy's constant, anguished crying and reported it to animal control. Animal control, in turn, paid a visit to the apartment, waiting outside until they heard the same anguished crying, thus giving them probable cause to enter the premises and discover first-hand evidence of what had been going on. The monsters were arrested and sent to jail. My guess is that they're probably out by now. I'd like to think they've somehow reformed, but I have my doubts.

Needless to say, Buffy came to me with her own unique set of issues. She was scared and distrustful. Understandably so. I knew it would be an uphill climb with Buffy, but I also knew that in time, with encouragement and love and a little bit of courage, we could work through the trust issues. We could work through any issues.

Buffy came home with me the same day as Betty Boop. I had visited the Anaheim shelter where Betty Boop was after spotting the picture of her online while searching for information about Gizmo's condition. I wanted Betty Boop but had no intentions of bringing home two dogs that day. But while waiting for Boop, Buffy was brought out. There was something about her that immediately caught my eye. She was beautiful and had an air of sophistication about her, even though she seemed a bit unkempt. I learned her background story from the woman who had been providing a foster home for her, and who had brought her in that day in the hopes of finding her a permanent home.

"So what's the deal with this one?" I had asked, smiling as I reached down and scratched Buffy's head. I simply had to ask; Buffy just didn't seem like she belonged in such a shelter. I sensed she was scared, but she was gentle and mannerly. It was surprising to think of her not providing some nice family somewhere with the pleasure of her company. I stopped smiling when the woman related the story.

Fortunately somebody had come along ready to adopt Buffy. But in the course of me filling out the paperwork for Betty Boop, I happened to mention I was a stay-at-home dog owner. The comment got the attention of the woman who ran the shelter. The person who was tentatively scheduled to take Buffy was a frequent business traveler and Buffy was obviously going to require a lot of attention, perhaps more so than what this person could provide. I was pulled aside and asked if I would have any interest in taking Buffy. "Well, I'm taking this cute little mutt here," I said, pointing towards Betty Boop, "and I have a pretty ill dog at home. I just don't think I could." Then I looked down at Buffy. "I mean, I couldn't. Could I?" I asked the question out loud but the woman could tell I was directing it to myself. I thought of the terrible life Buffy had lived to that point. I thought of the attention she needed, the attention she deserved. The life she could still have. The woman who ran the shelter wasn't saying anything. I'm sure she knew what I was thinking, and could probably tell by my face what my answer would be even before I had formulated it myself.

"What's one more dog?" I heard myself say at last.

Betty Boop and Buffy both came home with me that day and the two bonded instantly. It soon became very clear to me that Buffy was taking on a serious maternal role with Betty Boop. Much like me, Buffy has all the necessary emotional strength to be a mom but has never had the opportunity to give birth to any of her own. Thus she's taken on the responsibility of surrogate mother to those under our roof, even to puppies and smaller dogs around the neighborhood.

One day early on, I saw Buffy pacing and whining at Betty Boop's playpen. This went on for several minutes. It seemed odd but I quickly forgot about it. Just Buffy being motherly and protective, I imagined, but the very next day Betty Boop had one of her seizures. I didn't make the connection right away, but when the same thing happened the next time and the time after that, I came to realize that Buffy had an amazingly intuitive ability to know what's happening with Betty Boop, and an instinctual desire to want to summon help. Buffy's behavior became dependable enough that I'd cancel my next day's plans to be there for Betty Boop when she needed me most.

Mr. MaGoo tries to help with Betty Boop's seizures too, of course. He growls and barks and makes just as much of a fuss as Buffy, if not more so. Small difference: his warning comes *during* a seizure. And rather than a sincere warning, it comes across more like a grouchy, annoyed, protest. *Make it stop!* He seems to be shouting at me. But I know he means well. Thanks, anyway, Mr. MaGoo.

As for Mr. MaGoo and Buffy, they bonded the moment they met. With dogs, Buffy is like that—she trusts easily and is very comfortable around them right away. She's open and friendly, not a mean bone in her body. Buffy is love and beauty and kindness. And when Mr. MaGoo arrived on the scene, she was in heaven with another puppy to look after.

Humans are another story, and, with her history, predictably so. But through time and patience and care, Buffy has come to trust me deeply. She still struggles with strangers—especially those we come across outside of the house. I don't force her. I'll have anyone new hold out their hand. "When she's ready, she'll come to you," I tell them. It can sometimes take several days for Buffy to get accustomed to new people, but once she feels safe, it's all about love and attention with her.

I took Buffy to the groomer a month after I got her; her first real excursion out into the world of people since she'd arrived. She put the brakes on at the groomer's front door and wouldn't go any farther until I gently walked her slowly in, staying right by her side. We'll get there, I thought. Though she was distrusting of the groomers, she was beginning to trust me, and she must have sensed that I wouldn't lead her into a dangerous situation. Even still, it took almost another year before she started embracing trips to the groomers. Today she positively lights up. She delights in the bows above her ears that the groomer puts in and seems to almost glide out of the groomers, holding her head high in a most regal fashion. When she lights up, I light up too.

Buffy still looks to me for guidance and protection, even more so now that her sight and hearing aren't what they used to be. She often walks behind me now, using me as a kind of shield from the imaginary dangers of the sidewalk. With her diminished sight I'll sometimes have to pat the sidewalk to let her feel the vibrations, to let her know the sidewalk is still there and that it's safe to continue.

Despite Buffy's good nature and loving presence, she's had more than her share of physical issues. Often times physical problems manifest from emotional distress. This may very well be true for Buffy, given her past. But her love of rubber toys hasn't served her well either. I hadn't realized that while she was chewing them up, she was swallowing pieces which were tearing at the lining of her intestines. One morning I found her with severe symptoms of intestinal distress. I took her to Dr. Hilinski's office but after three or four days of IV antibiotics, a fever she was suffering wasn't breaking and her intestinal afflictions weren't subsiding.

Another veterinarian was consulted, one who specialized in intestinal problems, and Buffy was admitted to his facility where she had to spend several days and nights. Once again I found myself saying what had soon become my blank-check mantra: *Do whatever it takes, doctor!*

While Buffy spent time at the other vet's office, the rest of us went to visit her. Mr. MaGoo, as I recall, didn't at all like the idea of Buffy being there, unable to come home with us. "Vet-itis", as I think he put it, seemed to be his major concern. At any rate, we were soon able to bring Buffy home, all safe and sound, to much relief and happiness from the rest of the clan. Needless to say the rubber toys have been placed out of reach.

Then in 2004, Buffy began experiencing incessant panting in the middle of the night. Dr. Hilinski ran test after test, all of which kept coming back negative. But I wasn't satisfied. I knew something was wrong with Buffy and I challenged Dr. Hilinski to find out exactly what. "Something's not right," I said to him, and I repeated it: "Something's not right." Dr. Hilinski paused, looking down at Buffy with his arms folded and his hand stroking his chin thoughtfully. Finally he spoke.

"Let's get her to a specialist. There are a couple more tests I think we can run, but we need the specialist to do a proper diagnosis."

"Not that neurologist?!" I cried out, thinking for whatever reason that I was once again being referred to the neurologist that I had taken both Betty Boop and Gizmo to. Now, I had nothing necessarily against the man. Nothing logical or rational, that is. It's just that I never seemed to leave there with good news. He had given me two weeks on Gizmo and had recommended we euthanize Betty Boop, wanting her brain for science. I'm certain he's a fine neurologist. It's just that I think I'd rather take my chances somewhere else. Anywhere else!

"No, no," Dr. Hilinski chuckled. "It's another kind of specialist. He'll run a few tests, do some blood work and run a chemistry profile. Then maybe we can see what we're really dealing with." I breathed a sigh of relief and it was off to the specialist who examined Buffy and in short order began to suspect Cushing's Disease—an autoimmune condition often mistaken for signs of canine aging. To know for sure, we'd need to do another test. An expensive one. *Whatever it takes, doctor...*

The test came back positive. Back at Dr. Hilinski's office, the doctor admitted the findings were surprising. Buffy hadn't been exhibiting the usual signs and symptoms of Cushing's or those associated with aging. The truth is, by the time most people bring their dogs to their vets with

Cushing's the symptoms are much more obvious—hair loss, abdominal enlargement, increased thirst. And the truth is that by then it's often too late. We had apparently caught the disease relatively early, meaning we had the opportunity to get Buffy the proper medication, and hopefully add some longevity to her life. Dr. Hilinski offered me kudos for challenging him. For my part, I just trusted my instincts. It paid off. I've found it often does.

Dr Hilinski and his staff have come to discover that regardless of what's going on with any of my dogs, if they so much as throw me a single keyword, I'm online and researching. What I learned from the research I did on Cushing's Disease was that it's caused by two different kinds of tumors. One can be removed; one cannot. The choice seemed clear to me, but to remove it, Dr. Hilinski told me that a further test would be necessary to determine whether the tumor was even operable in the first place. "An expensive scan," he explained. *Whatever it takes, doctor...* Unfortunately the scan revealed that the tumor was located at the base of Buffy's brain, and consequently inoperable. Our only option was to give her medicines to help control the disease, medicines that it would be necessary for her to take for the remainder of her life. She takes Lysodren four times a week now.

Because of secondary health issues that often run concurrently with Cushing's, along with her advancing age, it's likely Buffy's eventual demise will be from something other than Cushing's, and I'm ever vigilant of symptoms that might indicate the onset of illness. Especially so since my research further revealed that most dogs with Cushing's Disease pass away within a two-year period.

I uncovered that little fact late one night, and sat looking at Buffy as she peacefully slept, unaware of her own condition, unaware that her time was running out. Unaware of my tears. Two years! It was Gizmo all over again. I felt heartbroken and discouraged. How could I go through it again, watching a beloved pet's health slowly deteriorate? How could I handle it, having to put another beloved pet to sleep? I thought of all that Buffy had been through in her life, and I thought of what she had come to mean to the whole household. I couldn't seem to stop crying. I didn't sleep and first thing the next morning I was on the phone to Dr. Hilinski.

"Kelly," he reassured me, "the two-year prognosis is for dogs whose symptoms are caught late. With Buffy, we caught it early. You know, you have to sometimes be careful with those Google searches of yours!" We both laughed and I immediately felt better. "Just continue with the medication," he added. No problem, I assured him. If there's one thing I've become expert at, it's responsibly delivering medications to dogs.

So far, two years has become six.

Though a survivor, more health issues are rising with Buffy's age. In 2010 she was diagnosed with transitional cell carcinoma. The cancer was found in her bladder and, once again, proved to be challenging. I was presented with three options: leave it, drain it, or remove it. There was no way I was going to choose to just leave it. I elected to have the tumor removed and tested. The test confirmed it was malignant for cancer.

While there is no direct link, it has been observed that Cushing's dogs often experience this affliction. Buffy also develops cysts that need to be checked and drained—on her hip, shoulder blade, and tummy. So far all the cysts have been benign. She now takes Metacam every day to help keep cancer cells from returning.

Although the entire cancer ordeal with Buffy has unavoidably brought back painful memories of losing Gizmo—the fear, the sadness, the tears, it's also brought on a new kind of determination. *This time I am stronger and wiser*, I say to myself. *This time I have a head start on the cancer cells and I have a plan.* After the diagnosis I bombarded Dr. Hilinski with questions. I am better equipped for battle than I was with Gizmo—I have more knowledge, better direction, a stronger resolve. And, too, modern medicine is more advanced than it was with Gizmo—there's more information, more effective treatments.

On the other hand, I am careful not to elevate my expectations beyond what is realistic for the long term. Buffy is now thirteen and I know she won't live forever. Every new day is a blessing. I know that's the right way to think about it, and so I try to remember that as much as I can. *Every new day is a blessing.* It's not a bad mantra for life in general, it seems to me.

Cocker Spaniels tend to be more prone to ear infections, too, so in addition to Buffy's medications for cancer and Cushing's, she gets ear drops three times per week and, because older dogs need to keep their eyes lubricated, drops in her eyes three times per week as well. Every six months, Buffy and I go to the vets for ultrasound and x-rays in an effort to keep a close watch on her condition. Though over time she's become more comfortable with Dr. Hilinski and his staff, she still prefers that I stay by her side.

Mr. MaGoo, unfortunately, has become grouchier and less patient with Buffy as she's aged. They're still very close but he'll often get in her face and lay on top of her in her bed. He grumbles to wake her up when I get home. I know he's just trying to help, as with her diminished hearing she often doesn't hear me enter, but frankly, he's sometimes not very nice about it. After four or five minutes of Mr. MaGoo's grumbling, Buffy will wake and come looking to me with sleepy eyes for hugs and kisses—trusting that I'll be there for her always.

Buffy continues to be a gentle motherly leader, setting a wonderful tone for the whole pack. She's definitely the sensitive, intuitive one of the group, and I've discovered it's rubbed off on me. Over time, Buffy's sensitive nature has taught me how to be more aware. It might have been that very lesson that had me paying closer attention to her early Cushing's symptoms and challenging Dr. Hilinski to find out what was wrong with her. It's interesting to think about—Buffy has taught me and, in turn, that teaching has helped save her life.

Buffy is loved, respected, and appreciated by everyone in our household. In addition to learning how to be more sensitive, she has taught me the importance of trust. And I have also come to understand what a little encouragement can do. Perhaps more than anything, I've also learned that in life there are no promises of tomorrow; I've learned to take more chances. Through me, Buffy has come to know courage but through her, I've had the courage to do more than I ever imagined. A few years back I jumped on a motorcycle for the first time. I found it to be scary, fun, exciting, thrilling, and empowering. And it was the kind of thing I'm not sure I would have had the courage to do had it not been for the example shown by Buffy. Beautiful, sensitive, courageous Buffy.

Chapter Nine

Cutie Cutie Carla Mae

Mr. MaGoo! Carla Mae "a raspy house guest"? This is no way for you to entitle a chapter about your sister. And what's with the chewed up yellow sticky notes all over the floor? Seventeen of them managed to find their way to my computer monitor, all of them with the same message: "Buy more doggie treats." Hmm...

For years before Carla Mae came along I thought my life was balanced and under control—complete. That's what I would've told you had you asked prior to May, 2005. I would've been wrong.

On a Wednesday afternoon in the spring of that year, I went to the grocery store where I ended up sharing some small talk with another dog owner as we both meandered down the aisle where the dog food was kept. Small talk became bigger talk when she revealed she owned and operated San Diego Pet Rescue, a small non-profit organization she ran out of her home. Gina was kind and friendly and shared the same passion that I have for dogs. She mentioned she was struggling with a fundraising event to promote pet adoptions. I offered her my business card if she needed some help with marketing. After all, I'd been doing online promotional work for a number of years and felt sure I could boost her web presence a notch.

Home later that night I decided to check out Gina's site. Navigating through it I saw an ad for a female Lhasa Apso with a horrific photo and a bio straight from the pages of Hell. *Experienced Lhasa Apso owners only!* I e-mailed Gina: "Good luck with this one!" Gina replied, saying she'd acquired Carla Mae from a pound in Los Angeles where she'd been visiting. She found Carla Mae cowering in the corner and felt especially sorry for her, telling the pound employee, "I'll take that one." It turns out that Carla Mae had been abused by her previous owner, verbally and physically. The owner had died and the owner's kids didn't want Carla Mae, opting to drop her off at the pound. It was no wonder. Gina described Carla Mae as "vicious." And now that she had her, she didn't quite know what to do with her.

Months passed and I gave little thought to the puppy with the tragic story who had caught my attention on Gina's site. Then in July, Gina called me from out of the blue. She reminded me about Carla Mae and said the dog had already gone through three foster families. "Kelly, you know the breed. Can you foster her? Just until I can find another home?" She sounded desperate. I reluctantly agreed, but only on the condition that Carla Mae would get along with Mr. MaGoo. "Bring her over, Gina," I said. "Let's see what happens." Mere moments later there was a knock on the door. Gina, who apparently must have called from no farther away than the corner, was standing there with Carla Mae in tow. I took Buffy and Mr. MaGoo outside to meet the new dog on what I was thinking was more neutral territory—a grassy area in front on my house.

Carla Mae didn't look like the same unkempt little dog I had viewed online months earlier. She was groomed and dressed up with bows. Gina happily introduced her with a hopeful look towards both me and Carla Mae. Gina and I nervously watched as the dogs "introduced themselves" to each other. Buffy, forever maternal and welcoming of other canines, appeared to have no problem with Carla Mae at all. More importantly, Mr. MaGoo seemed to bond with her almost instantly.

We all walked together through the garage. Carla Mae exhibited a lot of curiosity, sniffing the garage floor and taking everything in, but showed no signs of anger or aggression. We removed their leashes and allowed the dogs some time to scope each other out. Buffy appeared to be bored with introductions and trotted inside for a nap, thus essentially giving her stamp of approval and letting us know the excitement was over for her. Mr. MaGoo, on the other hand, kept a close watch on Carla Mae, seemingly fascinated by her every move. Eventually Carla Mae laid down on the floor and Mr. MaGoo scampered back in the house where he found Buffy napping and joined her in her bed, laying down on top of her head, as usual.

"Okay, Gina. She can stay until you can find a suitable home." We agreed that I would foster Carla Mae until August when we hoped to find her a permanent home through the San Diego Pet Rescue fundraiser planned for that month at the gym where I was teaching aerobics.

Notwithstanding hitting it off initially with the others, Carla Mae struggled to find her place in our daily routine. Walks were a challenge and feeding times were unfamiliar to her. She just couldn't seem to adjust to any kind of schedule. Goo soon ran out of patience with her, barking at her constantly. *Get on board or get out the door!* He seemed to be saying. Sometimes if Goo started barking directions, Buffy would follow suit. Now Carla Mae had three of us trying to get her in step with the household program. But she continued to struggle with the dynamics of our little family.

Carla Mae did enjoy attention, though, and was sometimes almost like a little child in the way she seemed to almost ache for it. But she just couldn't seem to understand why she had to stop what she was doing to go for a walk or eat, or anything else, for that matter. Gina had warned me about this; Carla would stubbornly refuse to do anything she didn't feel like doing. Gina had had her in training for this very reason. I was further warned that Carla Mae could actually be very aggressive in her rejection of authority.

So far, the rejection had manifested itself mostly as grumbling. At first, both Buffy and Mr. MaGoo perceived the grumbling as a physical threat, rather than just an act of non-compliance, which I gathered was what it really was. And often times Carla Mae's grumblings would be met with aggressiveness from the other two, escalating into fights that I would have to break up.

But by August of '05, I felt that Carla Mae had actually made a lot of progress in the months' time she had spent in our house. I'd been working with her every day since she'd arrived. She had become loving and trusting and I was confident she would make somebody a wonderful pet. I also knew that I was going to miss her.

Two days before the big fundraiser I was on the phone with my sister Colleen, Carla Mae curled up sweetly at my feet. I reached down to pet her and immediately felt her sharp little teeth piercing my flesh and chomping down hard into my hand. I screamed into the phone, startling not only my sister but the entire household—Buffy, Mr. MaGoo, and Betty Boop, the former two springing into the room to check out the situation. I hung up, grabbing tissues off my desk to try to stop the bleeding.

Buffy wasted no time. Coming to my defense, she lunged at Carla Mae. Mr. MaGoo did the same. All three dogs were growling and barking, each assuming attack mode. I knew that fur would soon be flying if I didn't jump in and take control. Then Carla Mae scurried off into the kitchen, backing herself into a corner where she was apparently ready to make a stand, the other dogs flying after her. I grabbed a child's gate I had on hand for such an event and quickly put it in place in an effort to separate the dogs. Goo was fiercely growling and trying to squeeze himself around the gate but, with some effort, I was finally able to snatch up both Buffy and Goo and usher them out into the garage.

Carla Mae meanwhile was standing her ground in the kitchen corner, baring her teeth threateningly, and ready for all takers. Had my hand not been bleeding and throbbing, I may have admired her tenacity, but as it was I had a class to teach in a half hour. I had no time to deal with the hand wound, let alone the mad dog that was in my kitchen.

I had to think fast. I wanted to approach her but I was in bare feet. I glanced over and saw my motorcycle boots by the door. I put them on. For good measure I put on my leather motorcycle jacket and gloves, too. Then I took a deep breath and stepped over the gate, slowly approaching the growling, snarling little demon. Carla Mae came at me with cobra-like quickness and accuracy. I snatched her up and held on tight. She continued snarling, trying to bite through my gloves. I clutched harder. I was not going to let go.

A minute passed. It seemed like an hour. Then Carla Mae let out a single plaintive cry and fell limp and still in my arms. It was over. She had surrendered. I kept holding her, gently then. And I continued to hold her, talking softly to her, until I could put off leaving for work no longer. I set her down lightly and made a quick phone call to Gina.

"Carla Mae isn't going to be ready for adoption." The words came out quickly. I described the scene, trying to put the best spin on it that I could, but on the other end of the line I heard Gina sigh.

"Well, you can't save them all, Kelly."

"What do you mean, Gina?"

"Kelly, you were her last hope. We have to put Carla Mae down."

I had minutes to get ready for work and told Gina I'd call her back after class. I kept the dogs separated, then dressed and left, Gina's words weighing heavily on my heart.

After class I called Gina back and tried explaining that the bite was not an act of viciousness. "Carla Mae has been nothing but entirely sweet. I've really made great strides with her. I think I just startled her while she was sleeping." Gina said it didn't matter; a bite was a bite. We continued talking and I was finally able to convince Gina not to put Carla Mae down. She agreed to let me work closely with Carla Mae, for at least a little longer. The fundraising event went on with great success and without Carla Mae. My hope was that we would still be able to find her a full time family, and I continued to work with her. Her surrender that day in the kitchen turned out to be a watershed event and from then on she became much more compliant. I never worried about her attacking again.

In the meantime, I'd been taking motorcycle safety classes learning to ride the new sport bike I'd purchased with the courage I had learned from Buffy. I had always been intrigued by bikes and had done my share of riding on the backs of them as a passenger. Now I'd decided to be the one gripping the handlebars, flying down the open road. It was a blast and I completely enjoyed it. After passing my motorcycle exam and earning my license, I continued to take classes and go for rides, around my neighborhood at first, but as my confidence and skill grew, the distance I was willing to travel expanded as well.

Weeks passed and I found myself gearing up for a track event. I was still painfully green, but my motorcycle pals convinced me the event would be a good opportunity to score some additional safety training that would most certainly go above and beyond what I had done to receive my license—entering turns, quick stops, advanced handling. Since I'd been having good luck and making progress with Carla Mae after the biting incident, I decided to take her with me. She turned out to be a model companion, taking to the road like a veteran traveler, and befriending the people at the track. We both enjoyed ourselves. I rode hard and by the end of the event really felt like a better rider. It was a wonderful trip.

But when we got back home, the trouble began again—little fights with the other dogs over toys, beds, and space. Carla Mae and I seemed to have come to terms with each other; I just wished she and the other dogs could do the same. There were struggles over territory and the struggles were beginning to get out of control. Full-scale fights were breaking out constantly. I was becoming especially worried about helpless Betty Boop, who was obviously no match for Carla Mae. I was at my wit's end and I knew I needed to do something quickly

In desperation I reached out to a local authority, a self-professed "expert dog trainer". I told the girl at the other end of the 800 line that I had fur flying daily, I'd been bitten, had a severely disabled dog in harm's way, and that I needed help. I was pleading with her. Help was available, the young voice informed me. Just as soon as I read the trainer's books, watched his training DVDs, and paid to attend at least one of his seminars. Until then I was on my own. Thanks for nothing, I wanted to say.

I hung up, tears of frustration running down my face. Clearly there was an overwhelming amount of work that was still needed with Carla Mae before she'd even be close to being ready for adoption. And the daily turmoil was rapidly consuming more and more of my time and energy, even money. I had volunteered to pay the vet bills and treat Carla Mae as my own so long as she would stay in Gina's name. In my mind, I was still considering Carla Mae to be very much *temporary*.

For the next couple months, Carla Mae continued to challenge my authority despite the progress I felt we had made. It was often one step forward, two steps back. She kept fighting with Buffy and Mr. MaGoo. She could be amiable and sweet, then suddenly a loud noise or a quick movement would set her off and she'd lunge at the other dogs. I needed help. I turned once again to my favorite veterinarian.

Dr. Hilinski suggested that I hover over Carla Mae when she was in "demon mode", as he called it. By so doing I would be acting towards Carla Mae like a mother or alpha dog, letting her know who the dominant one was. "Put a blanket over you when you do it, Kelly," the doctor advised, "for protection."

The very next day, when it was time to go for a walk, Carla Mae was having none of it—growling, baring her teeth, and refusing to comply. I decided to try Dr. Hilinski's method. I grabbed a blanket and bent down over Carla Mae, gently hovering above her. In no time she whimpered in apparent defeat and calmed down. It was a trick I'd wished I had learned months earlier. As time went on, I got even better and better results. Carla Mae was beginning to recognize me as boss.

There was still a ways to go, though, and after further consultation, Dr. Hilinski suggested I consider consulting with an animal behaviorist/communicator. "Not a dog trainer," he explained, "but more like a therapist for dogs." Why not? I thought. It certainly couldn't hurt. I found someone who started working with Carla Mae in late September. By early November the fighting was beginning to subside. And by Thanksgiving of 2005, there was finally peace in our home.

Strangely, I noticed a change in myself as well. I felt leadership qualities evolving within. I'd stuck it out. I took a difficult situation and made it better. My pack of high maintenance pups had become happy and manageable.

I thought of calling Gina in December to let her know how well things were going, but the holidays and the dogs and demands of my work left me with little time. I resolved to call her as soon as life settled down after the New Year.

All the dogs learned their place in the household and began to take comfort in their respective roles. Mr. MaGoo started warming up to Carla Mae and would try time and again to teach her to play. She didn't seem to understand and Mr. MaGoo would get visibly frustrated, but just before Christmas, while on a conference call, I turned around to see Carla Mae pawing back at Mr. MaGoo's playful boxing. The two were playing with each other.

It was late in January of 2006 when I finally sat down and called Gina to update her about Carla Mae. I felt Carla Mae was now ready for a permanent home. It would be tough to say goodbye, but I had done all that I had promised to do. My role in Carla Mae's life was over.

"I'm sorry," came the voice on the other end of the line. "Gina was killed in a car accident on January 12th. San Diego Pet Rescue has been dissolved." I sat in stunned disbelief. Gina had become a friend of mine. More than this, I had grown to admire her and her love for dogs. San Diego Pet Rescue was her baby, her pride and joy, and the work she'd been doing was priceless.

I sat quietly for a while after hanging up the phone. Then I looked down and saw Carla Mae at my feet. There was nowhere to take her now. Carla Mae was officially mine.

Not that I would've been able to give her up. I had already fallen in love with our "raspy house guest". Looking back, I knew when Carla Mae bit me; she was somehow mine to keep. *You picked your destiny, Carla Mae. I do wish you could've chosen a more gentle approach, but I suppose that wouldn't have been your style. And in so doing, you picked my destiny, too.*

Carla Mae is more accepting of meek, little Betty Boop these days, but remains cautious. I still don't leave the two alone together. Carla Mae and Mr. MaGoo now get along famously, with Carla Mae instigating playtime with Goo as often as he instigates it with her. She'll stand on her hind legs and imitate his boxing moves. She'll mimic the behavior of Buffy, too. Other times Carla Mae will engage in a little friendly competition with Buffy for my attention, nudging between Buffy and me as I'm petting Buffy. Carla Mae is clearly an alpha dog. Buffy is a maternal alpha. If Buffy follows me, then Carla Mae gets up and does the same thing. If one wants attention, the other will bully their way in. Of course Mr. MaGoo has no problem breaking in to remind us that it's really all about *him*.

Carla Mae has earned Buffy's trust and maternal care. Should Mr. MaGoo and Carla Mae start getting a little too scrappy with each other, Buffy will break it up. In the past she would've sided with and defended Mr. MaGoo without question. All three are her children now—Mr. MaGoo, Betty Boop, and Carla Mae.

Carla Mae still grumbles about things from time to time, but now, instead of taking an aggressive stance against it, Buffy and Mr. MaGoo walk away; they've learned her moods and know which ones to avoid and which ones I'll deal with myself. I've adjusted to the grumbling too. I've decided that Carla Mae will always push the boundaries to see what she can get away with. She's a dog who needs a strong, loving, and authoritative figure in her life and it's my everyday goal to be that figure.

Carla Mae is definitely an outside girl. She gets cabin fever if the weather keeps us from our daily walks. Two days inside and she's cranky, ready to pick a fight. Although she rejected a daily schedule in the beginning, she has now come to rely on it. When we do get out, she likes to be in front. I'm forever pulling her back to walk with me, not in front of me. She knows I'm in charge, but she still likes to test her boundaries. Mr. MaGoo struts beside Buffy, who stays loyally at my side.

On one early summer morning in 2009, about 5:30 A.M, Carla Mae was out back, in my fenced-in yard, enjoying the first break of day—rolling in the grass and watching for the sun to rise. Buffy and Mr. MaGoo were quick to do their business and come back inside, where I was. I looked out to check on Carla Mae and to my horror, through the morning darkness, saw several pairs of yellow, glowing eyes approaching. Other dogs perhaps? It didn't seem likely. A horrible, sick feeling came over me as it dawned on me I was looking at a pack of coyotes, one of which was stealthily scaling the fence no more than ten feet away from Carla Mae. I had heard plenty of stories about coyote's in the area; I knew they lived in the mountains behind the neighborhood, but I had no personal experience with them. Without thinking I ran out and snatched up Carla Mae, the coyotes watching my every move as I stole what they were hoping was their next meal. Turning and retreating back to the safety of our home, I slammed the door shut. It had to have been the fastest I've ever run. Inside I continued holding Carla Mae tight. I could feel my heart racing and I couldn't seem to stop shaking. Carla Mae, on the other hand, was just fine, never once realizing the danger she had just been in. I put her down and she scampered off to find Mr. MaGoo. Needless to say I'm now a little more careful when the dogs are outside. I stay out back with them and maintain a heightened sense of awareness.

Carla Mae is a real tomboy. The first time I tried to put bows on her I thought I'd lose my fingers. She seems to enjoy the bling a little more now and appreciates the pampering. Or maybe she's just willing to put up with the groomers for the car ride. Either way, trips there have become a treat for the whole family.

But even with the bows, Carla Mae can be outspoken and moody and grumpy. One must always approach her slowly and calmly. The abuse from her past has taught her to fear loud noises and sudden movement. When I discipline or even just call for her, I keep my voice low and calm. Anything else and she'll scurry away, taking a position in a corner, ready to spring into attack mode. It's disturbing to think of the abuse that has led to that instinctive response. I suppose she'll always react like that to loud noise. Crazy energy is okay with Buffy and Mr. MaGoo, but it puts Carla Mae in defense mode almost immediately. Yet Carla Mae warms quickly to strangers and adores attention.

All the dogs are still very territorial and Buffy and Mr. MaGoo definitely hold their ground with Carla Mae. Eventually she'll back down, grumbling as she does so. She was the only dog in her original home and hadn't been socialized with other animals. Although she's been with us for quite awhile, she still often prefers solitude. Going off by herself, especially when threatened, is her preference. I approach her calmly and quietly, hold her, and remind her that she's safe with me.

Today I'm teaching aerobics, kick boxing, and fitness classes, in addition to holding down my full time marketing job. I continue to ride my motorcycle, finding it a great stress reliever. I love and care for my dogs and feel like my life is more abundant and richer than ever before. And yet, I thought I had it all together before Carla Mae—a full and balanced life. Obviously I had more to learn. With Carla Mae I've learned leadership and assertiveness, qualities I use in other areas of my life. I'm a better manager and a better mentor.

I've also learned that second chances need to sometimes be followed by third and fourth ones, or however many it takes to follow in our hearts what feels right to us. Cutie Cutie Carla Mae—a precious, precious member of our little pack.

Chapter Ten

MaGoo Returns

WOOF! I thought I'd never get that human off the computer. It's purely ridiculous that I have to share a computer with her to begin with—PC: *personal* computer. Hello! I've not been able to check my e-mail for all of eternity. Forget about writing a book. And is it remotely possible that she takes a break and plays catch or spends a few minutes telling me how wonderful I am? Oh heck no.

The human has been on her very own little planet the entire time. It's absolutely amazing that medicines and bare necessities have been tended to at all. Oh sure, she's fed us and walked us, administered daily medications and cleaned up all of our messes. But get this—despite my gentle reminders to purchase doggie treats, the human seems to think being down to one, single, solitary two pound bag of doggie treats is somehow acceptable. I think the human would do well to tend to the canine catering and leave the writing to the pro—me.

And as for the three (count 'em *three*) chapters the human just finished writing—it looks like unadulterated balderdash to me. Talk about the Princess of Poppycock! *WOOF!* I haven't even bothered to read them. At a glance, it looks like she added a bunch of unnecessary details to my already perfectly brilliant work. I'll go back and read that nonsense when I need some insomnia material. Sorry that y'all had to wade through it.

I know you guys are aching to know what I've been up to. That's why you picked up this book originally. And who could blame you? I am an amazing animal. I'm fun. I'm entertaining. I'm freaking smart and way beyond your basic level of cute. It's a shame no one has figured out a way to clone me. Enough about me though. Let me tell you what I've been up against while the human was being a computer hog.

I was taking a nap and dreaming about cool grass and chasing butterflies when I woke to the sound of tap-tap-tapping on a keyboard. It was the human and it was sadly just the beginning of several days of much of the same tap-tap-tapping. I started off just trying to get the human's attention. I dropped my favorite squeaky toy at her feet. Nothing. I picked it up and gave it a couple more squeaks. Still nothing. I noticed that the sound of the telephone ringing diverted her attention and it occurred to me that perhaps that's when she's in *listening* mode, so I'd squeak the toy several times when she was on the phone. It became painfully obvious I needed to come up with ways to entertain myself.

I dug several trenches in the backyard, buried some bones and what looked like an old set of keys, tore up a couple pillows in a game of tug-o-war with Carla Mae, woke Buffy up on a dozen different occasions just to hear her grumble, knocked a bowl full of something gooey off the counter, got Carla Mae up dancing and then boxing, curled up with Betty Boop, then laid on top of her head, then ran to the window and barked at nothing in particular. Before I knew it, a whole hour had gone by and I was bored again. Boredom is not a good thing at all for me. It totally starts to bum me out. And then depression sets in and I become anti-social and unapproachable. I begin to lose the spark in my sparkle. It ruins my glad. Thankfully I live in a house full of maniacs and a neighborhood full of dogs and trespassers, so boredom never lasts very long.

The human doesn't ever seem to get bored, but there are times when she is definitely bumming. I'm hugely intuitive—there's not a mood or a particular energy that gets by me, so I know when she's stressed or sick or happy or whatever. Humans are more transparent than they realize.

There was this one time when the human's back was really bothering her, so when she laid down, I gently laid on top of her— applying warmth and pressure to the muscle spasms. The human thought it was a miracle I "sensed" her pain, but she'd been in pain all day—holding her back and walking funny. I'm a dog. I have eyes. I don't think it was any big mystery to anyone what was going on.

Another time, shortly after I'd heard something on the news about a SARS epidemic, the human started looking kind of gray and moving like her whole body ached. I watched her slowly manage to dole out meds and meals. It wasn't looking good for any of us. I kept a close watch on her. I could feel her elevated temperature practically from across the room, but stayed inches from her face nonetheless. Every time she'd wheeze in air, I'd bark and grumble and remind her to breathe back out. It was looking pretty grim for awhile. The human finally got up and left. My guess is she went to the vets like we all do when we're not feeling well. Dr. Hilinski must've had the right meds, because she seemed better when she got back home and was back to her normal self in a matter of days. Dr. Hilinski rocks that way.

Sometimes the human seems entirely lost and I have to direct her to the right room. I'll follow her up the stairs and then she'll just stop. Intuitively, I know the direction she wants to go and I'll dart in front of her and show her the way. She just shakes her head as if to say "What would I ever do without you, Mr. MaGoo?" Other times the human simply gets up and takes off for a specific room—in which case I dart in front of her and enter the room first to do a quick security check ahead of her. She definitely keeps me hopping.

When the human cries, I do my best to comfort her. Buffy and Carla Mae are never far behind me and of course, Betty Boop's heart is with the human always. We love that crazy woman. And while writing a book with her has been frustrating, I've learned a lot about her love for us and how this insane little group came to be.

I walked onto the job seeing a lot of work that needed to be done, a schedule to be enforced, security measures to be implemented, and morale to be uplifted. I think I got so caught up in my day-to-day activities, I overlooked the bigger picture. I failed to recognize that not only are these guys altogether blessed to have me in their lives, but I'm pretty blessed to have them in mine as well.

Much of my early years are a blur. I have memories of millions and millions of mother dogs and their pups—caged and in tight quarters. (Heck, that might be why I simply detest confined spaces today.) In our almost suffocating abode, there seemed to be a mix of love and abandonment; momentary joy followed by utter grief. I guess one could say I was bread from pedigree and born into chaos. The cycle was endless and an air of hopelessness permeated the walls. I curled up closely to Mom and rested in her care.

I don't remember humans playing catch or taking anyone on a walk or rubbing any bellies. Like I said, I don't really remember much. My first memory of a human was preceded by an unusual sound I later learned was called a "sneeze". Gloved hands quickly scooped me and my siblings up and away from our mother and into a cold box. The last sound I heard before being toted away was my mother crying. To this very day, the sound of anyone sneezing takes me back to that moment.

It occurs to me that might be why I enjoy laying on top of the human when she naps—she's like a surrogate mom to me. Granted a crazy, would-be-lost-without-me surrogate mom, but a mom I love nonetheless. It just sucks when she sneezes. I hate that sound. I feel like someone is going to snatch me up any minute. I probably should get over that. It would help if you humans could give us dogs a heads up, "Hey guys—I feel a sneeze coming on. Don't freak out." But it's like you hold them in till the last second and sneak up behind us and then let it rip. What's up with that?

The human's buttons can be pushed too and I like to keep her on her toes. *If not me, than who?* I love to play a game I call "No Dog's Land: Spy Game". Oh yeah. The couch is "no dog's land" and I am the stealthy spy who is constantly discovering new and different ways to occupy the hill/couch and capture the flag (or "remote control" as the human calls it). The top of the stairs is my watch tower and I am an observant and patient spy dog.

The human relaxes into the couch and waves the flag/remote control around—setting it down occasionally, just to pick it right back up again. Baiting me. Teasing me. Provoking me. I wait. The flag is set down. The human appears to be drifting off. I pounce! Down the watch tower steps, up on No Dog's Land! I snatch the flag and run back to the watch tower where I make the enemy's flag my personal chew toy. "Dammit Goo!" She yells as I celebrate yet another victory. The human is truly no match for me, but bless her heart, she keeps trying.

I observe everything. It's my job, it's who I am, it's what I'm about. I see a new spot or smell a new scent and I stop everything to investigate. Sometimes it takes a special effort on my part to communicate my findings to the human, but I'm pretty crafty so it's rarely an issue.

One day at the groomers, the technician cut one of my nails a bit too short. I hate it when that happens. Oh sure, it'll grow out. I still like all of them to be exactly the same though. I wondered how to let the human know about the imperfection and just as she rounded the corner, I began to limp. I even cried a little and held up my paw to show her the great injustice. She finally figured it out. The troubles I go through.

Don't get me wrong; we all think the groomer rocks. She's friendly and kind and attentive. Sometimes she runs a few minutes late and I don't hesitate to let her know this hasn't gone unnoticed. Manners are important to me and I think being late is rude. Still—I look *fabulous* when I walk out the front door. And with all the attention and increased media interest, a dog's gotta look his best.

Like I said, manners are important. In a dog's life, we have great reverence for "pecking order". It's considered rude and disrespectful not to abide by the established order. Entire books could be written on the intricacies of this time-honored process—the various complexities, difficulties, challenges, inevitable obstacles. It could very well be my next book: *MaGoo's Barking Order* or maybe *Order by MaGoo* or *Universal Order: What the World Needs Now.* I'll have to think about that one. For the purposes of keeping it simple, suffice to say there's a definite pecking order in our household. I am, quite obviously, the alpha male, protector and leader. Buffy is lady of the house and elder. I consider her my partner. Whenever we're out walking, my rule is beauty before muscle and I treat her as an equal and a lady with the utmost respect. Betty Boop has seniority, and while weak and frail, in the land of dogs, she out-ranks Carla Mae. I think Carla Mae still struggles with that on some level.

And then of course somewhere in the pecking order comes the human. I'm not exactly sure where. She seems to have this idea that it's *her* house. Yeah, yeah, I've seen the checkbook...I know all about the mortgage payments. But that's not the point. For what's a house without us? What would a dogless house be like? I can't even conceive of such a thing. Oh, it might be *technically* a house – walls, a roof, doors and windows and such. But it wouldn't be much of one, if you ask me. You see, it's like this: in the end, we could be living anywhere. A garage, a refrigerator box, under a bridge. No matter. As long as we're all together in the same place, we've got ourselves much more than a house. We've got ourselves a *home.*

Chapter Eleven

Something about Goo

Enough about the doggie treats Goo! They're baby carrots for Heaven's sake. That's why they're in the fridge and that's why two pounds is more than enough at one time!

While Betty Boop taught me patience on one level, every day I learn patience on quite another level with Mr. MaGoo. With Boopie, quiet is a good thing. With Goo, quiet means trouble. When Goo disappears and doesn't make so much as a peep, I know he's somewhere tearing something up (chewing on some designer purse of mine, for example) or making a mess or getting into stuff he has no business getting into. More than once I have found the contents of my gym bag strewn about the floor.

Or it might be that he's somewhere in the house experiencing depression or anxiety—in which case he licks and licks and licks his paws until they're nearly raw. For a dog, this is the equivalent of biting one's nails or twisting one's hair.

Goo has had this anxiety disorder since the first day I brought him home. I'll tell him "No lick!" over and over again. He'll walk away, into another room, out of sight, but I can still hear him. When I find him and say "no lick!" again, he'll just grumble; it does little to stop him. He's the least compliant of all my dogs. He's also the most animated.

Goo's anxiety disorder had me wondering, and still has me wondering, about his past. I became suspicious when I started doing some research on the breeder named in his paperwork. There was no website. There was no contact information or valid address. As far as one could tell, the breeder didn't even exist. Though Goo is genuine enough—a fully registered Lhasa Apso—exactly where he came from remains a mystery. I suspect, therefore, that Goo came from a puppy mill.

When I bought Goo I didn't realize the connection between puppy mills and pet shops. Knowing what I know now, I wonder if I would have even bought him in the first place. Not because of Goo, of course, but because of my unwillingness to want to support the inhumane practice of puppy mills. In a lot of ways, I'm happy I didn't know. Goo's loved and appreciated. He may not have ever been able to experience that otherwise. Because of his hard-headedness and anxiety, he stood a high likelihood of being misunderstood, possibly bounced around from agency to agency or from pound to pound. I'm so grateful Goo is mine. Thankfully he was not held onto for breeding purposes, and fortunately it appears he has escaped the birth defects commonly experienced in puppy mill dogs.

The ugly truth is that with puppy mills, profit margins can be big. And anyone can run one—most of the times they're set up in small confines with little to no start-up costs. Dogs are packed on top of dogs, often lying in their own feces, caged and unloved. Sanitary conditions are unspeakable and various infections are frequent. The dogs are there for one reason—to be bred and re-bred. They never know love, or even so much as a kind touch. And when pups are born they're often taken away from their mothers too early, to be sold for a quick profit. It makes me wonder if Goo's anxiety disorder is a result of some kind of separation anxiety. Goo might very well have been snatched away too soon from his mother, most likely an unfortunate dog housed in appalling conditions in a puppy mill somewhere with no other purpose than to continually breed more dogs.

The horror story that is the puppy mill industry has grown significantly, with organizations like the Humane Society (www.humanesociety.org) encouraging the public to report potential problems. The Society investigates tips and works diligently to end the illegal practice, but puppy mills are tough to locate and for many dogs, in those rare times when a mill is located, it's too late.

A recent example of a bust of a puppy mill in Mississippi shed some light on just how bad these places are. The Humane Society had fielded reports from people living close to a business operating as Sea Breeze Kennels. Sea Breeze had advertised puppies for sale over the Internet and in classified ads. The neighbors had apparently become concerned about the conditions at Sea Breeze and the Humane Society investigated along with the local Sheriff's department. What they found was sickening. There were over a hundred dogs, all being kept in terribly unsanitary conditions. A witness reported dog excrement just piled on the floors. The smell of urine was overwhelming. The dogs were crowded close together and flies were buzzing everywhere in the Mississippi heat. Two of the dogs were dead, and there was no telling for how long. The owner of Sea Breeze was charged with animal neglect. I wonder if it's enough.

It would be nice to think what the Humane Society shut down that day was a rarity. But for every mill they're able to bust, there might be dozens that they never find. Maybe hundreds. The truth is that these mills market themselves as respectable breeders and offer the unfortunate pups to unknowing (or maybe just unsympathetic) pet store owners and individuals at unbeatable prices. Using classified ads and the Internet, just like Sea Breeze, they operate well under the radar. As I found with Goo, it's nearly impossible to track down a puppy mill breeder once the sale is final.

Separation anxiety is just my guess, but it seems to be the most reasonable explanation. Whatever the source, Goo does well as long as he is getting attention, or something has his attention. But if he sits still for too long and gets bored, he begins licking his paws again. Some old habits die hard.

So it seems Goo is always in the middle of something—picking on Carla Mae, dumping every toy in the house at my feet, barking at random passersby. When anyone comes for a visit, he demands their attention and won't give up until he gets it. He *will* find a way. Boundaries are meant to be broken and rules are for other dogs.

I learned his preference for pushing boundaries early on, when he was no older than 12 weeks. Goo actually sought to expand the geographical boundaries of the house, squeezing himself under the patio fence and running loose and carefree through the neighborhood. It couldn't have been more than five minutes that my eyes were off of him, and it never occurred to me that it would be possible for him to squeeze out, but within no time he was clear down the block. When I discovered he was gone I went into full panic mode, running around the outside of the house and through the neighborhood, yelling, "Goo! Mr. MaGoo!" A neighbor heard my cries and came walking up to me with Mr. MaGoo in hand. "Is this what you're looking for?" she smiled. It was all of maybe two minutes from when I discovered Goo was missing to when the neighbor brought him back but it seemed like an eternity. I hugged Goo and thanked the neighbor and made a note to make the patio more secure.

Of course Goo will tell you that that was the exact point of his little demonstration.

The problem for me initially was that I simply wasn't used to the constant testing of the rules. Gizmo had never given me any such problems. She was the ideal turnkey dog, coming to me perfectly well-adjusted and perfectly well-behaved. Housebreaking was a snap and Gizmo pretty much went along with the schedule and the house rules with nary a protest. Goo was a lot more challenging, earning the nickname "Dammit Goo!" somewhere in the very first week of joining the household.

I realize, however, that a lot of the challenge comes from his intelligence. His propensity for breaking, or at least bending, the rules comes from an uncommon curiosity and desire to see "what happens if." On that level, I find myself at least respecting the motivations behind Goo's little transgressions. And the intelligence manifests itself in productive ways, as well, like when he grabs his own leash and brings it to me to let me know it's time for a walk. *Thank you, Mr. MaGoo*, I'll tell him. *Mommy appreciates your help.*

When it comes to respecting the boundaries with Buffy and Betty Boop, he's much more courteous and honorable—at least at meal time. He has respect for seniority and is more or less kind to his older sisters, if not just a bit impatient with them at times. Carla Mae has become his buddy and playmate and yes, low man on the totem pole, seniority-wise. Buffy and Betty Boop were members of the household before Goo and Carla Mae. Buffy gets fed first and Goo and Carla Mae have to wait. Betty Boop, of course, requires much more time to feed and care for, so I save her for last. If she were a less high maintenance pup, Goo would be waiting for her as well.

But then some days it seems like Goo is constantly in someone else's face—he'll push his way into Buffy's and Carla Mae's beds seemingly with no regard to their comfort whatsoever. He'll grumble at Buffy as she makes an unattractive noise and get grumpy if she doesn't wake up when he wants her to. He's perfectly willing to share toys, though—his toys, Buffy's toys, Carla Mae's toys, Boopie's toys; he's always ready to play.

Because Goo has a low tolerance for boredom and requires a certain amount of stimulus, I'll toss him a tennis ball while I'm working to keep him amused, or take an occasional five minute break to play tug-o-war with one of his toys. If I get too wrapped up in what I'm doing and neglect Goo, he'll remind me in no uncertain terms of his presence, either coming up to me and dropping a squeak toy at my feet (making sure I hear the thing squeaking, just in case I'm not paying attention), or by simply falling dramatically onto the floor in front of me, letting out a huge sigh of boredom, as though he's going to spiral down into certain despair if I don't drop everything I'm doing at that precise second and play with him.

Walks never fail to be interesting with Goo as he is extremely observant; every walk is a new adventure, another challenge. Often times I have to step up my leadership skills and remind him it's a *cardio* walk, not a police investigation, as he stops every two or three feet to sniff around and examine every bit of his immediate surroundings. When he gets on grass, it's a different story. He takes off, taking great delight in running through the grass, quickly getting a hundred yards ahead of us—only to dash back and attempt to grab one of the girls' leashes so *he* can walk them. My little helper.

Goo keeps a very close watch on me and even when he doesn't follow me from room to room, he definitely knows where to find me. The little guy doesn't miss a trick. And he seems to take a lot of joy in watching the other dogs look for me. He'll sit at the door to my office and hear Buffy get up or see Carla Mae making the rounds whimpering, looking for me, and he'll let them walk right by him as they go in the exact wrong direction—knowing full well I'm in the office. He sits and watches and appears to be entirely entertained by the whole process.

As for the groomers, Goo is quite the demanding little pup and begins commanding attention from the moment we arrive—generally fifteen minutes early. *She's not late, Goo. We're early.* Goo's manners still need a little work. As for the incident with his nails? A small nick turned into a big deal the moment he saw me, as he was being walked back to the front. Suddenly he went into fake limp mode, acting as though he'd lost a paw. My Goo— the drama queen. Sometimes it seems everything can be a "great injustice" to Goo. Did I say "demanding?" I think we could easily come up with 57 words and phrases to describe Mr. MaGoo's particular brand of demanding. His act was cute and pathetic at the same time and I had to reassure the groomer that Goo was just fine. All he needed was to be picked up and held by Mommy. It was just Goo, capitalizing on the moment, seizing another opportunity for attention.

Goo would have you think he's in charge—strong and rugged and independent. But when he's scared he runs to me to take care of him. Loud noises would have him jumping into my arms every time if I allowed it. The 4th of July can be bedlam around here. I try my best to ignore him so as not to reinforce the behavior—my way of saying that the noise will not hurt you, Goo. But it's hard to do.

Abandonment issues and separation anxiety continue to surface from time to time, but in comparison to everything Goo's sisters have been through and their physical challenges and disabilities; Goo's issues are easily managed. He's actually my "normal" dog, if there is such a thing. But even "normal" dogs can have their issues. In this, I suppose dogs are no different than humans. We all have our problems, some of them since birth, some of them acquired along the way. They manifest themselves in different ways, often resulting in abnormal behaviors, and often we're not even aware of them. I certainly have my own issues, and I try to remember this when I find myself being tested by Mr. MaGoo, or any of the dogs for that matter.

At least as humans we have the ability to try to become aware of those chinks in our armor, those emotional obstacles that hold us back in some way. I can try to make Mr. MaGoo aware of his paw-licking, for example, but at best all I can do is use reinforcement to try to discourage the habit. But that's not exactly total awareness. It's not like I can help him make the connection between his paw-licking and separation anxiety in an effort to help him resolve his past issues. Although sometimes I do find myself wondering. If ever there was a dog smart enough to reason himself through his own problems, it would be Mr. MaGoo.

Before Goo and his sisters, I had little idea that dogs labeled "high maintenance" could steal your heart just as easily as other dogs—maybe even easier. If anybody were to ask, I'd recommend the serious consideration of looking into a needier, more "difficult" dog. You can make a great difference in the life of such a dog, and the rewards can be immeasurable.

The sad truth is, there are hundreds of thousands of dogs that need homes—they're in temporary foster homes or rescue facilities or in pounds. They are full bred with papers, and they are mutts of unknown origins, yet just as sweet and just as deserving of a loving home. There are breed-specific rescue agencies and dog adoption specialists who are ready to help you find a suitable pet. After years of being actively involved in pet rescue and adoption, and after seeing all the dogs I have seen in just my small corner of the world, I can't imagine anyone not being able to find the dog of their dreams through a rescue agency. Whether it's a German Shepherd or a Lhasa Apso or a Cocker Spaniel or just a dog that needs loved, the ideal pet awaits.

Of course one can't be given a guarantee that the adopted dog will be capable of writing a book like Mr. MaGoo. But either way, Goo's certainly right about one thing: the right pet (or pets as the case may be) can turn an otherwise ordinary house into a sweet and loving home. Sometimes crazy, sometimes noisy, sometimes even maddening. But always, a home.

Chapter Twelve

Goo's back behind the Computer!

Wow. Such detail about my life as a puppy! I get that I'm entirely interesting, but dang—can we stick to the facts? How in the world does the human even come up with this stuff? Puppy mills? For real? As if you humans could be *that* cruel. I mean, we've seen some examples of cruelty around here—I'm thinking about Buffy's story, for example—but these are rare, right? I mean, you humans can't be *that* bad. Honestly, maybe the human missed her calling to be a horror writer. Shoot—I dunno. Maybe she just woke up one morning and thought she was Stephen King. Or else she just likes spreading rumors and lies. I honestly have no idea. Did y'all know that humans are the only species who lie? The rest of the universe sees lying as a terrible waste of oxygen. But back to me...

The fact of the matter is, I don't have a boat load of memories from my puppyhood and what I do remember is chaotic and bleak and hardly "book worthy." But a puppy mill? That's plain crazy. Really my first full-blown memories are of the pet shop where the human acquired me. (Best day of her life.) Everything before that is a bit hazy. But what's past is past. Let's talk about today! Let's talk some more about my adorable cuteness and awesome intellect. That's what ya'll wanna hear, right? Oh, and pay no attention to the human and her wildly fictitious stories about "paw licking." Another false invention. She's just trying to create controversy. Trying to sell more books no doubt. She's – oh, boy, here she is, speak of the devil...

Sorry, Goo. I just have to jump in to set the record straight. Your continued denial about the paw licking isn't helping. It's time you faced the facts. You're a big dog now. But I will agree to stop talking about your past. I just thought it was important to bring to everybody's attention the tragic truth about puppy mills.

Then it's true?

Sadly, yes.

But how can humans be so cruel to animals?

I don't know, Goo. Humans are even cruel to other humans.

I'll tell ya, you humans are a strange lot. This is why the world is run by dogs. Can you imagine if humans ran the world? Can you imagine the problems we'd all be facing? *Woof!* Crime, wars, pollution—all those things I see on that silly TV show you watch every night. It would suck.

We have all those things, Goo. That TV show is called "The Evening News." Unfortunately, the world is run by humans, and I'm afraid sometimes we don't do a very good job.

Run by humans! Ooh, that's rich. Keep believin', sister. I think everybody reading knows the true score. We let you think you're running it. The truth is, behind every great leader is a strong dog. Typically, in fact, an adorable Lhasa Apso just like me. *Woof!* Tell ya what, though. I'll give you credit for the stuff on "The Evening News." Ya'll can take the responsibility for *that*.

Okay, but aren't you getting a little sidetracked, Goo? This was supposed to be a chapter where you kind of wrap things up, wasn't it?

Hey, I was doing fine until you butted in and hijacked it. I was focused. I was determined. I was in a zone. Now I'm all flustered and there's only one thing that can re-focus me: doggy treats.

I'm sorry I butted in, Goo, but you're not getting any doggy treats. You have work to do. We have to finish this book. We have to –

Doggy treats! Doggy treats! Doggy treats!

Stop it, Goo! You'll wake up Buffy. She needs her sleep.

Yeah, yeah, yeah, Buffy always needs her sleep. I'll tell you what Buffy needs. She needs more playtime with yours truly. What dog in their right mind wouldn't want more playtime with me? *Woof!* Same with Carla Mae. Same with Betty Boop. Well, maybe not Betty Boop. Strange one, she is, but a cute, little thing. I'm afraid I'd crush her if she joined me for playtime. Then I'd get in big trouble. I'll tell ya, you don't want to get in trouble with this human here. She'll lecture and talk your ears off. Sometimes I think she just likes to hear herself talk. I don't know why. It's not as if a human voice is beautiful or anything. I mean, it's not like a bark, which of course is the most pleasing sound in the universe, depending on the bark, of course. I have a nice loud *Woof!* Which sounds regal and bold. I've noticed other dogs have more of a "yap" or even a "yip." Yaps and yips aren't very regal or bold-sounding. They're even worse than "arfs" which can actually be kind of annoying. I'm not sure why some dogs yip while other dogs yap and still other dogs arf. It's one of those mysteries of the universe, I suppose. I'm just grateful that I was bestowed with a *"Woof!"*

Speaking of animal sounds, what's up with the "moo" thing that cows do? I'd be embarrassed if I opened my mouth and all that came out was a "moo." You know what has a nice sound? Birds. It almost makes me not want to chase them but, dang it, I just can't help myself. They're just so….chase able. They sit there looking all cool and calm and they start singing and acting like they're celebrities or something and it's just so much fun to lunge towards them and see the look of surprise on their little beaked faces and watch them get all scared. Then of course they fly off. Stupid birds. As if that's fair. As if you can just fly off. How is that fair? I could fly, if I wanted to. But I don't have wings…

Goo! You're way off track again! Focus!

Right, right. Focus. Okay, where was I? Yes, yes, I remember. The human wants a wrap-up chapter. A summary. Okay, let me start summarizing by revisiting this "wing" issue. In wondering why dogs don't have them, I have come to the conclusion that God, in His infinite wisdom, probably decided we would be way too perfect if we had wings, thus creating enormous insecurity in all of the other animals. The world would be rampant with tremendous feelings of inadequacy. And then where would we be?

Goo!

Okay, okay, okay. I know. Summary chapter. Summary, summary summary. You know, "summary" sounds a lot like "summer." I love the summer. All but the 4th of July, that is. Now I noticed the human wrote about that troubling holiday in the last chapter. She just had to go and tell you all that I don't like loud noises. What she didn't tell you was that my hatred of all things loud has nothing to do with *fear*. Not at all. What it is, is that loud noises scare the *other* dogs. And in my concern for the other dogs, I often like to empathize with them by pretending to be scared myself. It's a little trick I learned that seems to make everybody feel better. It's called "psychology." Maybe the human would know that if she ever bothered to…I don't know…read a book some time, perhaps?

Goo!!!

Woof!

Goo, it occurs to me that you're not ready to focus on any more writing just now. Why don't we do this: let me write the wrap-up chapter. And then, if you behave and you can focus yourself again, I'll let you have some last words after that.

Can I have some doggy treats in the meantime?

(Sigh.) Yes, Goo, you can have some doggy treats in the meantime.

See, everybody? Is there really any question as to who's in charge around here?

Chapter Thirteen

Reasons

You know, the more I think about it, the more I wonder who really is in charge. Ten years ago I used to think I had it all together. I was master of my fate, captain of my soul. But if there's one thing I've learned in the past ten years, it's that the universe has a strange way of humbling masters and captains. We move along in life thinking we're in control, thinking we're maybe a little smarter than the next person, making what we think are intelligent decisions and steering our lives towards ends of our choosing.

Then, just when we think we've got it all together, along comes a Gizmo moment. And everything changes. Looking back, it's reasonable to ask whether I consciously chose Gizmo that day long ago when I spotted her in the pet shop window, or if Gizmo really chose me. In fact, it's more than just reasonable to ask. It's necessary, I think, that we look closely at our lives for the clues that tell us where we should be going, or maybe even who we really are. Who chose whom that day? And why?

It's clear to me now that there was a reason I happened to glance up and look in that window. And I can go even further back and think of earlier events in my life that seemed, at the time, random and disjointed. My time with Shawn. My experience with horses. I learned important things in those years—things like how to be loving and patient—qualities that would be necessary later. I couldn't see it at the time, but those experiences were seeds that would eventually sprout into something alive and vital—a more developed, more mature *me*.

With Gizmo I learned unconditional love. Gizmo was there for me through good times and bad. I always had a friend and a confidant in Gizmo. Somebody who never questioned me, somebody who always accepted me—accepted my moods, accepted my laughter, accepted my tears. But nothing comes for free. Strangely, even unconditional love can have conditions. My payment was in the despair I felt with Gizmo's brain cancer diagnosis, and the grief I felt in her death. But there are lessons to be learned in those things, too. Always there are lessons. Always there are reasons.

Acquiring Betty Boop and Buffy was even more seemingly random and unplanned than acquiring Gizmo. And yet I think of the valuable lessons my experiences with those two have taught me, and continue to teach me to this day. Unplanned? It seemed a total fluke that I would end up with Betty Boop. There were thirty-five people ahead of me in line for her. Thirty-five people had expressed interest in adopting her. For one reason or another, each and every one of them opted out. Some found other dogs; some changed their minds after meeting Betty Boop and discovering her special-needs condition, and some just never showed up. I didn't know it at the time, but there were reasons why Betty Boop was destined to come home with me. Always there are reasons.

With Betty Boop, I have learned tremendous patience. It's almost hard to remember what I was like before her. Thirty-minute wait at a restaurant? Forget it. A line of people at the bank? Intolerable. Traffic? Traffic might have been the worst. I was quick to anger and not very bashful about…expressing myself. Let's just describe me as a "colorful" driver and leave it at that. With Betty Boop the world has slowed down. There's no need to rush. There never was, actually, but I just never knew it.

She has also taught me what unconditional love really means and that it works both ways. I gratefully return the unconditional love that my dogs offer me. Sometimes it's hard. Sitting with Betty Boop for thirty minutes or more twice a day to feed her isn't what I'd always like to be doing. But unconditional love means unconditional. And when you stop and think about it, isn't that what *love* really means? Is it really love when we start qualifying it, attaching restrictions and stipulations to it?

With Buffy I have learned sensitivity. Her gentle, intuitive, motherly ways have influenced how I interact not just with the other dogs, but with other people, too. I think back to the time I challenged Dr. Hilinski to dig deeper to find what was wrong with Buffy, feeling it in my very soul that there was something yet to discover, and I realize that Buffy has taught me to trust my instincts, taught me to look inward for answers, or at least clues to life's mysteries.

She has also taught me that every day is a blessing. I don't know how much longer I will have Buffy, but I am determined to enjoy each day to the fullest, to appreciate the moments as they pass.

With Carla Mae I have found leadership qualities within that I did not know I possessed. I have learned that I can overcome even the most difficult of circumstances. I shudder to think how close Carla Mae came to being given up on. I was her last chance. But sometimes a chance is all that's needed, if somebody is willing to provide it.

And Mr. MaGoo? Mr. MaGoo continues to teach me new things seemingly every day. I never stop learning the lessons of patience and understanding with Goo. And he keeps me on my toes, keeps me off-balance. Just when I think I've got it all figured, he'll pull off something that makes me realize I don't have it figured out at all. Maybe more than anything, I have learned that being off-balance isn't a bad way to be. We're all off-balance anyway; we just don't realize it most of the time. But by accepting the unpredictable nature of life, we become more flexible, more adaptable.

Life's unpredictability also teaches us humility. It keeps us in check, keeps us from yielding to arrogance. In some way, each dog—Gizmo, Betty Boop, Buffy, Mr. MaGoo, and Carla Mae—has reminded me that I remain an unfinished work. There is always something new to learn and there is always room for growth and development.

All of these wonderful animals have come into my life for different reasons. I could never really tell what those reasons were at the time, nor did I even know there *were* reasons. I remember sitting on the kitchen floor with Betty Boop on those first days with her, crying in frustration, trying desperately to feed her. Why? I wondered. Why was God doing this? In time the reasons became clear. I imagine it is this way with anybody who has lived long enough to be able to look back at certain things that, at the time, seemed random and painful. By virtue of hindsight, from the more objective perspective that time elapsed surely always provides, the dots connect. The randomness suddenly doesn't seem so random. The plan begins to become revealed. This is the true miracle of life.

Overall, with all of the dogs, I have learned the real meaning of words like loyalty and commitment and dedication. You can't successfully run a household of special-needs dogs by doing things in a careless or casual way. You have to do things right. You have to do the best job that you can do all of the time, not just some of the time. You have to devote yourself to it. This kind of commitment has helped me in every other area of my life and in every other relationship that I have in my life, whether personal or professional.

I was not always thus. When I think back to my time before Gizmo, I remember a young woman who was fairly scatter-brained, with no real direction, no clear purpose, nothing to be devoted to. The dogs have grounded me, they have matured me. In a sense, they have domesticated me. Isn't that ironic? As humans we credit ourselves for domesticating certain animals, dogs chief among them. And yet in my life I have found that the dogs have domesticated me as much or more than I have domesticated them. Or perhaps the domestication has been equal. And therein lies the beauty of the relationships I have had with each of my dogs—the relationships have been mutually fulfilling.

And so what does the future bring? I try as best I can to live in the moment, to not look too far ahead. I try to have faith that God has taken me this far and will continue to take me as far as He has planned. I may not understand the inevitable twists and turns, but I have faith that the course before me will become clear, that there is a reason for everything. Always there are reasons.

I try not to think of the eventual loss of my dogs. Dogs don't live forever. Buffy in particular is facing an uphill battle that may play itself out sooner rather than later. If I'm to be honest, I have to admit that most of the time I live in denial about the ultimate fate of the household. When I do think about it, I try to just revel in the time we all still have together, and the times we've already spent. Each morning I check on Betty Boop, watching for the reassuring movement of her little chest as she sleeps, rising and falling as her lungs fill up with air to let me know that we have another day together. And I say a prayer of thanks. Her prognosis of having, at most, one more year to live, was made almost ten years ago.

I imagine, sometimes, my life in, say, ten or twenty years. Maybe there will be a man in it. Somebody understanding and kind. I have had too many disappointments to count on that, however. But either way, I do know that there will always be a dog in the household. Perhaps not a special-needs dog, and certainly not a puppy. I'm thinking that as I grow older, my preference will most likely be for an older, more settled dog.

But no matter how many dogs I ever have, I will never forget the dogs that make up my current household. I will grieve with the loss of each and every one, but I will try to remember the good times and I will treasure the memories. I try to remember the words of Anthony Hopkins as C.S. Lewis in *Shadowlands*, reflecting on the eventual loss of his one true love: "The pain then is part of the happiness now. That's the deal."

If there are lessons that I have learned that are specific to me, there are also more general lessons that I am grateful I can share. I would tell anybody who asked to find what it is within you that lights your passion. Follow your heart. If you quiet yourself and listen, you will learn the direction to go. God speaks to us always, if we just take the time to listen, if we just trust our intuition, our gut feel. And once you know what is right for you, then have the courage to go for it. Stick up for yourself. Don't allow yourself to be bullied. Be assertive.

Watch, too, for the inevitable distractions. There is much in our society that is likely to throw you off course if you allow it. Material comforts and escapist entertainment are no substitutes for the real things that make up the fabric of a life well lived. The chase for money. Drugs, alcohol, casual sex. All of these things can actually take us further from the path we are meant to be on, and the pressure to conform can be enormous. Perhaps the hardest thing of all is to remain true to oneself.

But no matter how difficult something might be, as big an obstacle as you might some day find before you, you can overcome it. I had no idea what I was capable of doing before the dogs of my household became a part of my life. I would not have thought myself able to handle them. But I have learned that you never know just how strong you can be until your strength is really called upon.

If this all seems to be about more than just dogs, that is not an accident. There are life lessons in everything. For me, the lessons have come to me primarily through my dogs. They have been conduits, if you will. Messengers, in a sense—each one delivering another piece of the puzzle, leading me further and further into understanding. From where come these messages? That's the question. I laugh sometimes when I consider what DOG spelled backwards is! In your life, you might have completely different conduits, completely different sources of wisdom and understanding. But the sources are there, just waiting for you to pick up on them.

I'll leave it for the reader to decide who chose whom that day when I spotted Gizmo in the window of the pet shop. I have my own ideas. I can say this with certainty, however: my life has been immeasurably enriched by the company of Gizmo and those who have followed—Betty Boop, Buffy, Mr. MaGoo, and Carla Mae. I am a different person because of their presence. And they will always be a part of me. I know that there will come a time when they will be only memories and I will grieve. But I also know that that sadness, too, will be a part of the journey, a part of the lessons. Always there are reasons. That's the deal.

Chapter Fourteen

Reasons Schmeasons

Okay, kids, hang on a sec. I just finished reading the human's last chapter and I need to collect myself. I mean, I've just got something in my eye, okay? No big deal. Probably just dust from the human's inattention to simple household cleanliness. Sheesh, how is a dog supposed to function in this environment?

All right, look, I appreciate the human's perspective but, as you may have already guessed, mine is quite different from the human's delusional point of view—sweet and loving though it is. I believe the reason for this book is to share with you all the absolute joy of owning an amazingly cute, ferocious, brilliant, entertaining, loyal, respected security expert such as myself. We've learned that while not all Lhasa Apsos are alike, we are a magnificent breed and one certainly worthy of great praise and admiration—a gift of the most royal magnitude. Noble and reputable.

We've certainly learned as well that not all *humans* are alike. I mean, let's face it. Some of you are simply not worthy of having a dog. Some of you are complete idiots—clowns that continue to leave a funny taste in my mouth. There. I said it. I hate to be so gruff about it, but what other conclusion can I come to? I know, I know—I should forgive. But I still have some anger issues going on and some of the people described by the human in this book I'd like to just chew up and spit out. I pray for God to give me the ability to forgive these dirt bags one day. Until then, I really like the idea of chewing them to shreds. I'll probably go upstairs and take my frustrations out on a piece of the human's furniture. That always helps. And it tastes good, too!

As far as Gizmo goes, I didn't really get the point of that whole, big, long story at first. But I guess the human falling for a puppy in the window is what started the whole thing. It all led to my being here, so I guess Gizmo must have been an okay dog after all. I still think the human spent just a bit too much time on her, though.

And while we're on the subject of Gizmo, what's the deal with the hat? Why don't I have a hat? I think I would look rocking awesome in a new hat. Something slick and stylish—maybe a Dick Tracy look going on. A cool fedora, you know? But in blue or black or maybe gray. Though I definitely could go for a white hat. I could actually use a different color for every day of the week or one for each of my many jobs—writer, security expert, entertainment professional, finest friend, perfect companion, fearless leader, peerless organizer, profound motivator, dazzling defender. I do wear a lot of hats figuratively; why not literally?

Hey, you guys should totally do an e-mail campaign to the publisher suggesting a calendar featuring pictures of me in glorious dog hats! Dog hats I would, of course, be allowed to keep. It could become my thing. Imagine me showing up for book signings in one of the hats I modeled for the calendar! It's no secret I'm destined for greatness. I might as well gear up for the increased media attention and bask in the limelight while the getting is good. Think of all the doggy treats I'll be able to buy! *Woof!* It's good to be loved.

In regards to Sparky—yes, he's a real dog in our neighborhood and a real pain in my butt. That goes double for King. The difference being that Sparky may actually read this one day while I'm quite positive King is completely illiterate and remains clueless as to the purpose of books. So no worries kids; the big, ugly German Shepherd is not going to come looking for me because I called him an imbecile and a social retard. Big stupid head. It's good to be a writer! *And in your face Sparky! I'm not afraid of you!*

I've also learned that no one being, canine or otherwise, can be all things to all others. With the exception of me, of course. We need others around us to kind of fill in the gaps. Even Sparky serves a purpose—he's there to help me keep my security skills sharp. And I'm in his life because the dog obviously needs someone to ride his tail on a daily basis. King is around so I have someone to make fun of, and he gets someone making fun of him, even though he's a bit too stupid to realize it. So—all things, ya know.

It's my personal belief that Betty Boop came into our lives as the purest form of love. She has shown us all the very power of love and patience and acceptance—and the miracles one need only sit still to experience. Our greatest thoughts, ideas, and inspirations come not to us when we are hurrying through our busy lives, but when we simply sit still long enough to enjoy a moment. Betty Boop reminds us all that love is indeed a precious thing and well worth slowing down for.

Beautiful Buffy may not have turned out to be the energetic playmate I was looking for, but I found something else in her I didn't even know I needed—a partner, helpmate, and maternal figure. She's lovely and graceful and hugely protective of the household at the same time. I've seen her in action defending both the human and Betty Boop. Don't be deceived, Buffy can kick some serious butt when she wants to. It's just a shame she can't get those walking farts under control. But what do I know? Maybe that's what makes her look like she's almost gliding when she chases birds. Shoot, maybe it's good to have gas.

Carla Mae was such a raspy, mistrustful, angry, aggressive little cuss in the beginning, it pained me to call her a fellow Lhasa Apso. But she's turned out to be big fun! She's a first-class dancer, putting a lot of tail in her strut. *Shake it, shake it, but don't break, ba-by!* And she's not a bad boxer either, though her wrestling skills aren't quite up to my level. I'm okay with that. It's good to play and have fun.

The human, quite frankly, is a nutcase. And so I honestly believed I was brought into this household to bring order to an otherwise chaotic environment, to keep the property and inhabitants safe, to provide levity and entertainment. But I can see now that the human does bring more than doggy treats to the table in exchange for my services. The doctors, the medicines, the grooming, the toys, the kibble—it all takes money. The human is a complete and total meal ticket! It's good to be a kept canine.

I know the human wrote some drivel about not having us forever and one day... blah, blah, blah. Look, we're all just fine. Really. As I sit at my desk and type out the last few words of my first (but certainly not last) book, I can see Betty Boop napping, Buffy playing kissy face with the human, and Carla Mae is right here aching to play with yours truly. We're all together and all is exactly as it should be. You know, you humans spend entirely too much time fretting about tomorrow when today has barely begun. And the human called *me* a drama queen. Seems to me she's projecting her own personality a bit, yes?

I hope you all have learned a few new words through this literary experience. I have great appreciation and respect for the English language and have found the onset of the Internet to be a direct attack on spelling and grammar and vocabulary. I even find myself forgetting the rules sometimes. So I challenge you to learn a new word every day and devote some time to expanding your vocabulary, perfecting your grammar, and working on your orthoepy—that's the study of correct pronunciation. It's good to be intelligent and well spoken.

Well kids, it's been way fun to share with you the glory and pure joy that is me. Drop me an e-mail sometime. Send me a new hat. I'll get to the tons and tons of fan mail as fast as my four paws will allow me. I'm still fighting with the DMV for a license, so don't be surprised to see the human with me for book signings. She's my chauffeur until I get this mess straightened out. I'll be traveling with my trusted posse—Buffy, Carla Mae, and Betty Boop as well. They'll want to be close by and the girls will *love* being a part of all the hoopla. I feel certain there'll be plenty of attention and excitement to go around—share the wealth, ya know? I might even let them hang out in my dressing room when the movie production begins. We'll see. You know how temperamental directors and producers can be.

For now, I'm off to play some with Carla Mae, scare up a few doggy treats from the human, go for a walk, chew on Buffy's ear, and then take a nap. Who knows what lies beyond that? It's sure to be something interesting.

It's good to be me.

The End

Epilogue

I sat in the parking lot, trembling, unable to get my legs to work. Finally, after several deep breaths I managed to calm myself enough to get out of the car and walk into the veterinarian's office. "I'm here to pick up Betty Boop," I said, fighting back the tears.

Two days earlier, I had brought Boopsie into the unfamiliar office. Thirteen days before that, I had completed my move, 500 miles away. I had an opportunity to advance my career and personal life with the move, and the timing felt right. Just before we pulled up roots, I had taken the whole household into Dr. Hilinski's office one more time for a thorough check, and had said goodbye to the doctor and his wonderful staff.

A couple weeks later, on a quiet Saturday morning, Betty Boop had unnerved me with a horrific bark while I was giving her a bath. So strange was the sound that Carla Mae, who had been close by, ran out of the room and hid. I held Boop and tried to calm her but I could tell that something was seriously wrong. I instinctively checked her gums and saw that they were an unhealthy, pale white color.

The situation threw me into semi-panic mode; I had no veterinarian in my new town as of yet, but I knew Boop was in need of medical attention. I did a quick online search, found a veterinarian nearby, and off we went. In the meantime I had managed to get a hold of Dr. Hilinski who was good enough to fax Boop's most recent medical records to the new vet. Boop was put on oxygen immediately when we arrived and the doctor promised to monitor her closely, reassuring me, and telling me they would call me with any news.

At about noon, she called, telling me the recommendation was to have me take Boop to a specialist. They were having problems oxygenating her; she had developed aspiration pneumonia. Her little lungs had performed loyally for ten years, but they were failing her now. In a conversation with Dr. Hilinski later, he would tell me that aspiration pneumonia presents a life-threatening struggle even for an otherwise healthy, 80-pound dog; Betty Boop weighed between three and four pounds and, of course, was not otherwise healthy.

I drove to the vet's, ready to take Boop wherever she needed to go and do for her whatever I could do. But in the twenty minutes it had taken me to drive there, the situation had changed. Betty Boop's condition had deteriorated and had apparently reached an irreversible point. The doctor was telling me it was time to say goodbye.

My mind was swirling and I heard myself pleading. Money is no object, I kept saying. I was sure if we just took Boop to the specialist, she would be all right. I even suggested taking her to Dr. Hilinski who could perform whatever treatment was appropriate. I would drive the five-hundred miles with Boop on my lap.

"Kelly," the doctor said, "She'd never survive the journey." I sat down, rocking back and forth, crying. "I'm very sorry," continued the doctor, "but the situation is such that there is nothing more that can be done. She's a fighter, Kelly. But her little body is giving out. It's time." Deep down I knew the doctor was right. She sat down next to me until I could finally muster the strength to stand and she ushered me to the back room where Betty Boop lay, oxygen mask over her face as she struggled for what would be her last breaths.

"Mommy's here," I whispered to her, my tears dropping onto her little frail body. I picked her up, held her, kissed her. She snuggled into my arms, her little oxygen mask pressing in. She had been through so much in her ten years. She had defied the odds and had made a mockery of her original six-month diagnosis. I was so proud of her. I told her that as I held her; told her that I loved her, told her she was my hero.

I asked for a clipping of her hair and then the doctor asked if I was ready to sign the paperwork for them to proceed. "I'll never be ready," I said. And then I signed. We moved to another room where I was able to sit with Boop, talking gently to her and crying, finally allowing the doctor to administer the first shot. Instantly I thought of Gizmo. I remembered going through this before. And I wondered if it was the right thing to do. Were there really no options left? I thought about pleading with the doctor once more, but instead just whispered to Betty that she would always be my Boopie Bear, and then I nodded to the doctor who administered the final shot.

She went quietly, peacefully. I sat with her as long as I could, but then I had to leave, had to leave without her.

Two days later I was sitting in the parking lot of the vet's office, ready to pick up Betty Boop for the final time. Over the course of those days I had imagined that I had come to grips with the loss of Betty Boop. But as I sat there, ready to go in, the finality of the situation suddenly hit me and I found myself overcome with emotion, trembling, tears flowing freely. My Boopsie was gone.

Betty Boop had taught me so much. I was a different – better – person, having had her in my care for the past ten years. I had learned patience and I had learned unconditional love. She had inspired me with her enthusiasm for life, in spite of her physical difficulties. Her life teaches me still. Inspires me still. Carla Mae has been diagnosed with a cataract that will eventually cost her her sight. Betty Boop has taught me about blindness, has readied me for the days ahead with Carla. In addition, if you recall, Buffy was diagnosed with cancer March 2010. Well, I just learned that her tumor has grown and multiplied throughout her bladder and down her urethra tube. I have been told, two months at best; my days will be comforting her. Of course, I am being hopeful, I have been told in the past a certain time period and my dogs have surpassed and beaten the odds.

As I sat in the car that day, I thought about a poem I had once read entitled "Rainbow Bridge." The author is apparently unknown but it's a poem about a place "just this side of Heaven" where our pets wait for us. It's a place of sunshine and hills and meadows. I imagine Betty Boop there. She's running now, no longer walking in her tight little circles, but running freely through the grass, eyes wide open, taking in all the sights and all the colors.

I made it out of the car that day and began walking towards the vet's office, ready to pick up the earthly remains of my Betty Boop, but knowing in my heart that she was now in a much better place. And Gizmo is there too, of course, leading her, showing her the way. They're chasing butterflies, I imagine.

~ Kelly Preston, March 7, 2011